The Youth Worker's
PERSONAL MANAGEMENT HANDBOOK

Edited by
Lee Sparks

The Youth Worker's
PERSONAL
MANAGEMENT
HANDBOOK

Copyright ©1985 by Thom Schultz Publications, Inc.

Library of Congress Catalog No. 84-73152
ISBN 0931-529-03-4

Designed by Jean Bruns
Illustrations by Laurel Watson—Pages 21-23
Jacket Photo by Dick Kezlan

"How to Get Along With Your Senior Pastor" (page 135) is reprinted
from THE COMPLETE YOUTH MINISTRIES HANDBOOK, VOL. 2—
CATCHING THE RAINBOW by J. David Stone. Copyright ©1981 by Creative Youth Ministry Models. Reprinted by permission of the publisher, Abingdon Press.
"10 Commandments for Good Listening" (page 43) is reprinted from For
Parents Newsletter, May-June, 1981.

Contents

SECTION 4
Managing Your Self

Contributors

Dennis C. Benson
Rich Bimler
Paul Borthwick
Charles Bradshaw
John Cassis
Mary Lou Conway
Daryl Dale
Ken Davis
Roger Dill
Bobby O. Edwards
Tom Franks
Jim Green
Jim Hancock
Cindy S. Hansen
Bob Haughey
David R. Helms
Ginny Ward Holderness
Larry Keefauver
James C. Kolar

Roland Larson
Roland Martinson
Cindy Parolini
Gary Richardson
Margaret Rickers
Russ Ritchel
Joani Schultz
Thom Schultz
Ben Sharpton
John Shaw
Donald M. Somers
Tim Smith
Bill Stearns
J. David Stone
Paul Thompson
Rich Van Pelt
Sandra Wilmoth
Bill Wolfe

Preface

You.

This book is for you.

Who are you?

You are a dedicated youth worker. Perhaps you are a full-time youth minister. Or you are a youth ministry volunteer. You may be a Christian education director or an ordained pastor. Or you are none of the above, but you are involved in youth work.

Whatever your involvement, you are serious about your ministry. You care for kids. You want the best for them. And you want to give them the best you possibly can.

That is why **The Youth Worker's Personal Management Handbook** is for you. This book is not a curriculum, nor a thrown-together gimmicks collection, nor a pedantic theology. This handbook's purpose is simple: To help you manage yourself so that you will enjoy an even more effective youth ministry.

This handbook's 30-plus contributors offer *decades* of experience to help you manage the four major areas of the youth worker's life:

1. Managing your relationships with young people: management principles for relating with youth, finding and meeting their needs and solving common youth group problems.

2. Managing your relationships with adults involved in youth ministry: how to work with and support your volunteers, church staff, parents and senior pastors.

3. Managing your family life: practical suggestions for balancing your ministry's demands and your family's needs.

4. Managing your self: helpful ideas for managing your priorities, spiritual growth, time, self-esteem, money, creative gifts, health, stress, organizational skills and career decisions.

Most of these chapters have appeared in GROUP, the youth ministry magazine. The remaining were written specifically for this handbook. The authors are dedicated youth workers in a wide range of ministries with kids. And they care for you, the youth worker. God be with you as you strive toward excellence in youth work.

Lee Sparks

Section 1

MANAGING YOUR RELATIONSHIPS WITH YOUNG PEOPLE

What are the marks of an excellent youth ministry? Here's how one youth minister applied concepts from the best-selling book "In Search of Excellence" to his youth ministry.

CHAPTER

1

In Search Of Excellence For Your Ministry

BY TIM SMITH

"**I**f there is any excellence and if anything worthy of praise, let your mind dwell on these things." (Philippians 4:8b, NASB)

"That's a nice fluffy bun," I thought to myself as I bit into my 17th Big Mac for the month. I'm amazed at McDonald's worldwide consistency of product and service. If I'm in my hometown or in Tupelo, Miss., I know what I'll get and how I'll be treated by the employees. McDonald's seems to have patterned itself after Philippians 4:8 (above). I think their corporate minds have dwelt on "things worthy of praise": consistency, cleanliness, friendly service, quick response. McDonald's reward: billions sold.

I'm not saying McDonald's is the ideal. But we youth workers can learn several lessons from better-managed businesses such as McDonald's. Why not work toward a ministry that is characterized by quick response to people, practical innovation and a team commitment to shared values?

But ministry isn't quite as simple as frying hamburgers.

Recently I returned from a week of camp with our senior high students. On my desk were the usual, familiar greetings:

"Call Mildred, re: personal problem with daughter—please call today!"

"Emergency! Please respond immediately! Bill Parker broke leg—visit him in hospital today—he's very low."

"Please complete report by 2 p.m. for the Church Board's Tuesday night meeting."

YOUTH MINISTRY EXCELLENCE

Who wants excellence? I'm interested in survival! How can I even think about quick personal responses to people's needs when all I want to do is go home and rest? And how can I take time to be "practically innovative" when I have been running on five hours of sleep?

I needed time away alone. So I packed my Bible, notebook, appointment calendar and picnic chest and took off to the mountains.

I spent a few hours studying the scriptures, praying and planning. Then I pulled out the book we were reading and discussing as a pastoral staff, **In Search of Excellence**, by Thomas J. Peters and Robert H. Waterman Jr. It was in the Sierras that I first discovered some of this book's possibilities for youth ministry. It reminded me of some of my observations of McDonald's: close to the customer, discover your niche, productivity through people, build a team.

CLOSE TO THE CUSTOMER

I know I'm in trouble when I begin to look at people as interruptions. Remember the time when you only had a few hours to prepare the Bible study and one of your least favorite humans popped into your office "just for a minute"? It seems trivial to say a minister must be close to people. But **In Search of Excellence** reminds us: "A simple summary of what our research uncovered on the customer attribute is this: The excellent companies really are close to their customers. That's it. Other companies talk about it; the excellent companies do it."

To be close to people in our care means we must listen to them; we must be sensitive to their needs. Do you have regular time when you can simply listen? Is there space in your week for being "close to the customer"?

Spending quality time with people doesn't mean you have to spend hours with them. It means you are offering, to the best of your ability, what the person needs for that time. To put it in a business sense, "You are servicing the customer." If people ask for something you cannot offer, tell them so and follow up quickly.

For example, a guy in our high school group came up to me and asked, "What book can I read to get me more into God? I'm having trouble with the book I'm reading."

"What are you reading now?" I asked.

"It's by some guy name 'Toraz' or something like that," he responded.

"Do you mean A.W. Tozer?" I asked.

"Yeah, that's the guy. He's a little too heavy for me."

"I can see why. Most sophomores would find Tozer hard to read. But here are some names of some authors you can check out at the bookstore."

I gave him a few names and checked back with him. He said, "I have this good book. It's by this guy named R.A. Torrey. He really nails it to you about commitment."

"That's great, Steve. I'm glad you got it. I've read him and he's super." Of course I didn't tell Steve I read Torrey in seminary, not high school.

In our church's youth ministry we actually have staff assigned to caring. Their responsibility is to determine areas of need in the lives of young people and respond personally. These caring people don't have to do programs or teach; they simply use their gifts of mercy and service to meet needs.

DISCOVER YOUR NICHE

According to **In Search of Excellence**, the best-run companies have effectively developed their "nichemanship," which has helped them stay close to the customer: "The customer orientation is by definition a way of 'tailoring'—a way of finding a particular niche where you're better at something than anybody else."

I find this concept liberating. I get tired of trying to compete with other ministries (and other pastors on our staff). I'm not sure why I do such silly gymnastics. But I do know one thing: When I concentrate on what I do well, I feel less threatened. It's important to define your mission.

If you are gifted in campus work and evangelism, then don't spend a lot of time doing small group discipleship and leadership training. Find people whose "niches" complement your talents. We all know this is biblical:

"I say to every man among you not to think more highly of himself than he ought to think; but to think so as to have sound judgment, as God has allotted to each a measure of faith. For just as we have many members in one body and all the members do not have the same function . . ." (Romans 12:3,4, NASB)

Determining your niche helps you exercise your spiritual gifts and natural talents. It helps you prioritize time, finances, staff and other resources. It aids you in saying "no" to the many demands, comparisons and comments that might sidetrack you.

I am convinced if we can target a group and really meet its needs, then we can spread out to include other groups. Presently in our ministry we are concentrating on meeting the relationship needs of college students. Many have moved away from home to attend our local university. Many collegians feel "orphaned" and enjoy being "adopted" by a church family even if it's for dinner one night a week. Eating in a home, instead of a dormitory or apartment, is quite encouraging for many students.

But when I first came to the church, our "college" group had only 30 percent college students in it. About 40 percent of them were in their mid- to late-20s and about 30 percent had never gone to college or had been out for a year or two. Our problem: How do we minister to a college group of non-collegians?

We realized that we had an opportunity ("niche") to minister significantly to college students. They were our primary group to reach. But we had to minister to the others too. So we used Peters and Waterman's observation that the best-run companies experiment; they try new ways. We discussed this problem with our singles class; they warmly welcomed the "older collegians" into their group. Six months later a group of college graduates asked me to help start a "career class" for post-college people. We began with a Bible study and later invited all the post-collegians to leave the college class and join the newly designed "early career" class. We are now able to target the university for Christian students who need fellowship and growth.

PRODUCTIVITY THROUGH PEOPLE

"Ministry would be easy if it weren't for people," I thought as I ended a long, draining day that was full of "interruptions." I'd forgotten that ministry is people. Correspondence is important. Planning is crucial. Cleaning off my desk is helpful. But the respect for the person must be the top priority. In their book, Peters and Waterman reinforce the scriptural principle of respecting the person: "There was hardly a more pervasive theme in the excellent companies than respect for the individual. . . These companies give people control over their destinies; they make meaning for people. They turn the average Joe and the average Jane into winners. They let, even insist that, people stick out. They accentuate the positive."

They also found employees of best-run companies view the firm as an "extended family." Also, each company had a "razzle-dazzle" campaign in which the employees worked toward a goal, achievement or honor.

A genuine respect for the individual reflects an accurate appraisal of the activity of God's grace in our lives. We can achieve extraordinary results through ordinary people when we include the remarkable grace factor: "For by grace you have been saved through faith; and that not of yourselves, it is the gift of God; not as a result of works, that no one should boast. For we are His workmanship, created in Christ Jesus for good works, which God prepared beforehand, that we should walk in them" (Ephesians 2:8-10, NASB).

The penetrating truth about grace is that it is personal. When I come to realize that Christ died for me, and is concerned about having a relationship with me, I can then begin to comprehend the value God holds for the individual.

My personal ministry struggle is meeting the needs of individuals within the group. Instead of adding up the needs of individuals, I often assume the needs of a few and multiply them by the number of remaining people. By doing this, I show a lack of sensitivity for the majority of the people in my group. It's easy to base our decisions on the needs of those closest to us. But the ones who may need it most, get the least attention.

In order to meet this need, our ministry has five phases: cultivation, incorporation (evangelism), edification, service and restoration. I spend time once a month with a student who represents each phase. That way I receive personal input on how we are ministering to the diverse needs of students. "Restoration" is the phase that includes people who have "slipped out the backdoor." What better way to show respect for the individual than to say with a personal visit: "Hey, where have you been? We miss you."

BUILD A TEAM

Leadership training is another way to show respect for the individual. It says: "I want to help you grow as a leader. I want you to be influential." Leaders' self-esteem grows as well as their feeling of team spirit. Leadership development allows a more personal ministry with students because there are now more trained people to evaluate and respond to the diverse needs of other young people. Thus, we have now become "close to the customer."

Ray Kroc, the founder of McDonald's, valued the individual's contribution: "A well-run restaurant is like a winning baseball team. It makes the most of every crew member's talent and takes advantage of every split-second opportunity to speed up service."

A well-run ministry makes the most of every member's talent and takes advantage of every opportunity to improve service to the individual. Take time to read the fourth chapter of Ephesians to recapture the emphasis on "team-ness." The oneness that Paul encourages is possible when we preserve "the unity of the Spirit" and use our gifts. To respect the individual, we youth workers need to place people in roles that best utilize their gifts; we need to equip them for success.

One of the most helpful catalysts for team ministry is a leadership retreat. We have three or four leadership retreats each year. At these retreats we concentrate on relationship building. We set goals as a team, and together we assess our progress from our previous goals. There is time for creative suggestions or alternatives. We take time to celebrate. We praise God for what he has done and thank him for what he'll continue to do. These retreats help the team members remember that they are significant and needed. They assure continuity in personnel and planning.

At these retreats I find some way of rewarding or acknowledging their faithfulness: take them out for pizza on the retreat; buy them a book; write personal notes of appreciation; create silly certificates of merit such as "Worst Water Skier," "Achievement Award in Culinary Arts" (cooking hot dogs), "Carl Rogers 'Uh-Huh' Counseling Certificate" and "Human Lobster Certificate" (worst sunburn). When people feel good about themselves, they feel free to use their talents to meet the needs of others.

THE DECISION FOR EXCELLENCE

I returned to McDonald's to continue my search for youth ministry excellence. This time I brought my associate and daughter, Nicole. Immediately we were greeted with: "Good afternoon. May I serve you?" We had been in the restaurant only 30 seconds and already we were being served. Now that's being close to the customer. The place was packed with college students and preschoolers who brought their parents along to pay for their lunch. Nicole and I ate a good meal for a reasonable price and then we headed outside to McDonald-land, a playground of plastic fries, burgers and fish sandwiches. They really have thought about people—little people. Then I realized McDonald's is the only place that has these playgrounds. They have discovered their niche. As Nicole bounced on a french fry, I thought, "Ministry is finding a need and filling it with quality service." With Christ we have the quality product—we need to provide quality service.

In my pursuit of excellence I've found that those who win are more willing to give than get. They're concerned about the other person. They know the more they give, the more they receive. Winning is relatively simple, but it is not easy. We who minister to youth have a choice to make: Are we just getting by? Or are we striving for excellence?

ADDITIONAL READING

In Search of Excellence, Thomas J. Peters and Robert H. Waterman Jr., Harper and Row.

Megatrends: Ten New Directions Transforming Our Lives, John Naisbitt, Warner.

Are you in step with your
kids' world? To com-
municate with youth, you
need to understand what is
important to them.

CHAPTER
2

How to Keep In Touch With Needs of the Youth

BY JIM HANCOCK

Nothing starts a meeting off on the wrong foot like arriving late. Especially if you're 20 years late.

I once attended an extravagantly titled high school gathering, innocently expecting a good time. I was disappointed and so was my youth group.

Not that the ministry idea was bad. The evening featured an outstanding speaker I had wanted the kids in my group to hear. The publicity had been out for weeks in advance. We had high hopes.

But the meeting itself was carried off in poor style. The organizers did it just like it would have been done when they were young. It would have been a hit in the 1960s, but decades later, it died. The leaders' memories were too long, the kids' too short.

The evening was a nightmare of aged songs, cornball jokes and syrupy introductions. The kids were confused by songs they had never heard and/or didn't like. The speaker had to dilute his message to meet the different needs of the wide age range of kids who attended. And there was a number of adults in attendance, enough to neutralize the feeling that it was a "youth" meeting.

I don't question the sincerity of the people who planned and "executed" that meeting; however, they produced an experience that was boring, awkward and badly paced, simply because they tried to do it like it was done when they were kids.

THE WAY THINGS WERE

A major news magazine reports that people remember in a significant firsthand way what has happened since they were 10 years old; but little or nothing before that. If you accept that, you acknowledge a severely limited historical memory for the kids in your group. The things you and I remember as if they happened yesterday are vague recollections to today's kids, if they recall them at all.

Think what that means. The high schoolers I work with don't remember for example: Vietnam; the moonwalk; Watergate; the Watts riot; the Chicago riot; Kent State; the assassinations of John and Robert Kennedy and Martin Luther King; the Beatles (a 14-year-old was overheard asking incredulously, "Did you know that Paul McCartney was with a band before Wings?"); the music of Woodstock, Peter, Paul and Mary or Bob Dylan (Dylan won a Grammy in 1979; I couldn't find a single kid who knew who Dylan was); or the deaths of Janis Joplin, Jimi Hendrix and Jim Morrison.

Those events and people shaped and shook my world in the 60s and 70s. But that was all over by the time my present youth group members became alert to the world around them.

THE WAY THINGS ARE

All this has special meaning to me as a youth worker.

First, I must stay current. To communicate with kids, I must speak in terms and events which are meaningful to them. A sign on the wall at Decision magazine reads: "Put the hay where the sheep can reach it." That's the principle. I'm committed to do whatever is necessary to feed my young flock. What I know about Peter, Paul and Mary matters little unless I know at least something about popular recording artists of today. Profound recollections of the Nixon years won't substitute for awareness of what's happening in the current presidential administration.

Secondly, I've got to grow spiritually. Admittedly, most of us do ministry as we've seen it modeled. If our models were good ones, we're safe—to a point. That point is reached when I serve up stale content and programs. Effective youth work is fresh. It lives for both the youth worker and the kids.

That freshness requires two disciplines. The first is simply doing my homework. In reading and being with kids I look for the new angle, the fresh idea, the alternative approach and new ways to communicate biblical truths. I pick my colleagues' brains, have lunch with others in my field, and attend conferences and seminars. I do my homework so I can stay fresh.

The second discipline is absolutely necessary: I work at growing in intimacy with God. I need to reflect the fact that our creative God is doing something in my life and in my ministry. While I'm growing spiritually, my kids get the benefit of my personal freshness. I invite kids to walk a road that I've already begun. My continuing growth reassures them that it's worth the trip.

THE END OF THE MATTER

Keeping current is a matter of responsibility and caring. I want to do my job well. That means growing—staying fresh.

I know that, in the end, I help kids grow by making the faith a live option in their world, by being there, alongside, when they need me.

I want to be sure that when the help arrives, it's on time.

14 TIPS ON KEEPING CURRENT

● Pick a happening—sporting event, concert, swimming party, youth group meeting—and just sit back, listen and observe. What sorts of things do young people talk about? What are their gripes? What are possible explanations for their actions?

● Find out what radio stations young people in your area listen to and spend some time listening to them. Pick up a list of the "Top 40" hits at a record shop and listen to the top four or five.

● Ask the kids in your group to bring their favorite record, play it for the group and explain why they like it.

● Find out what magazines your young people are reading and read them yourself. If you're not sure what kids read, check with the school librarian. Same for popular books.

● Analyze the advertisements in youth-oriented magazines and on radio shows. What are the products being advertised and basic needs to be met?

● Find out what movies your young people are watching, then watch those yourself. Try to figure out what made the kids want to see the movies. Do the same for television.

● Spend a little time in the library reading about the mental, physical, social and psychological characteristics of teenagers. Then keep those characteristics in mind as you plan.

● Find a successful and respected teacher who has been around awhile. Ask the teacher how he or she relates to the kids, what sorts of needs they have, what they react to best and how today's kids compare with kids a few years ago.

● Attend an event or activity that draws huge numbers of kids. Watch and listen. What things are happening, how is the program designed and how do the kids react to the event?

● Involve young people in all stages of your planning. Let them provide input on items such as the format and agenda of meetings, retreats and events.

● Subscribe to the high school newspapers.

● Find someone who has had an effective youth ministry for 10 years or longer. Talk about ministry ideas and young people. Get his or her experienced perspective.

● Read the "News, Trends and Tips" section in GROUP Magazine. You can subscribe by writing to: GROUP, Box 481, Loveland, CO 80539.

● Really get to know the people in your group. Look for those times when little special is happening—when everyone is hanging around and talking about nothing in particular. Don't feel that you have to be the super leader and dominate the conversation. Follow the flow of the conversation. Listen to what everyone else is talking about.

ADDITIONAL READING

The Private Life of the American Teenager, Jane Norman and Myron Harris, Rawson-Wade.

Teenagers Themselves, compiled by the Glenbard East Echo, Adama.

Test yourself on these basic youth ministry questions and compare your answers to those of a noted youth ministry expert.

Quiz Yourself On Youth Work

BY ROLAND MARTINSON

Editor's Note:
We asked Dr. Roland Martinson, researcher, youth ministry expert and professor at Luther-Northwestern Seminary in Minneapolis, to provide basic answers to the questions. Check your answers with Roland's. If you agree, great! If you disagree, think about the various answers. What's the disagreement? Enjoy thinking through these answers.

YOUTH MINISTRY QUIZ

1. When it comes to having charisma with kids, I'm most like (circle the figure that best describes you):

OTHER:
(Sketch your own)

2. **The following diagram best describes the relationship between kids in my youth group and kids who attend my church's services, but not the youth group (circle the diagram that represents the relationship):**

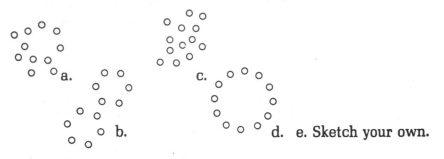

a.   c.

b.   d.   e. Sketch your own.

3. **Most people in my church think young people (check those that apply):**
- ☐ should stick to themselves.
- ☐ are the church of the future.
- ☐ should be involved in the church's day-to-day activities.
- ☐ are the church of today.
- ☐ are cute.

4. **"Youth ministry is no different from other ministries in my church" (circle the appropriate answer to this statement):**

                    True   False

5. **When it comes to relating to the kids in my group, I'm most like (circle one):**

6. Youth ministry is best led by (circle the one that seems most appropriate):

7. The following statement best describes the role of young people in my church (choose one):

☐ Adults plan for the kids and the kids do it.
☐ Our kids plan and run their own ministry.
☐ Adults and kids plan and carry out the ministry together.
☐ We set up situations that put young people and adults in relationships with each other.
☐ Adults act as baby sitters in our youth group.

1. When it comes to having charisma with kids, I'm most like:

Many churches believe in the Pied Piper philosophy of youth ministry. That is, if you find the right person with the right stuff, responsibility for youth ministry belongs to him or her.

There's merit in involving someone whom kids like to be around. God has given some people the gift of working with kids. But we can't leave youth ministry there.

It's important that the pastor or priest be an integral part of the church's youth ministry. In Search Institute's "Ten Faces of Youth Ministry," the No. 1 quality people want in their pastor is a symbol of faith to whom they can point and say: "There. There's one in whom I see God working among us." The pastors need to indicate that they value, care about and understand kids.

Trained, caring lay leaders are essential too. Youth need adults to remind them, "You're special!" One of the church's powerful roles is providing faith models who are supportive, thinking, leading people. Youth ministry needs adults.

Youth ministry ceases to be led by a Pied Piper or hero when it's a congregationally owned ministry. Youth ministry is by people: pastors, adults and the youth themselves. Until youth ministry is planned, organizationally developed and done, it will not be integrated into a congregation; it will simply take place on the edge.

2. The following diagram best describes the relationship between kids in my youth group and kids who attend my church's services, but not the youth group:

A congregation's youth ministry isn't simply those kids who are active. It's not just those kids who go on a trip or come to youth group. Every kid in the congregation is part of the youth ministry.

I remember Gary. He was a genius, pock-faced and greasy-fingered kid who worked on lawn mowers at Rocky's Hardware. He never came to youth group events, but I talked with him while he worked on lawn mowers—just to get to know him. About six months after my first visit with him, he appeared in my office saying, "I've got to talk with you!" Gary was struggling with a friend who was on drugs and pilfering the till at work. He wanted to help his friend and felt I was someone he could trust. Gary eventually started coming to church. Even though he never got involved in youth group, Gary was a part of our church's youth ministry.

3. Most people in my church think young people:

"Someday they're going to be in charge. *Someday* they'll need to know what to do. *Someday* this church will be in their hands. We must get them ready for that day!"

This misconception applies especially to the decision makers of the congregation. As long as kids aren't viewed as real Christians who are fully alive now as the body of Christ, they won't be a respected, vital part of the church.

As a teenager, Jesus asked questions in the temple, standing toe to toe, eyeball to eyeball with the teachers of the church. Kids ask questions too: "What's God all about? What does faith have to do with me and my life?" Young people aren't the future church. They're a vital part of the present church with marvelous gifts to give.

During one of my visits to the local high school, one of the students invited me to her band class. Of the 72 kids playing horns, 23 of them belonged to our church. Being a pastor of a church that harbored an old mortuary organ, I invited those 23 kids to the parsonage for a jam session. Three weeks later, their brass ensemble accompanied the opening hymn. The congregational singing turned around. The teenagers became our musical leaders.

Young people have gifts to give! We can tap those gifts and start integrating them into the life of the congregation.

Some churches have a youth Sunday one day a year. The youth bring in guitars and the church "puts up with all that stuff" for one day. Contrary to that idea, every worship service should have a place for teenagers. One of the finest places to include kids is in the sermon. The illustrations, rather than reflecting negatives about teenagers, can draw upon the positive. Kids will go away saying, "Hey, our minister knows us and values who we are."

4. Youth ministry is no different from other ministries in my church.

Kids have a unique life stage coupled with unique gifts. We need to understand that uniqueness and integrate it into the life of the congregation.

Youth ministry costs money and takes time and effort. Buildings, funds and training programs reflect high priorities. Staff time and money need to be provided for youth ministry to happen.

5. When it comes to relating to the kids in my group, I'm most like:

He was half-dead, a lumpy guy with a squeaky voice. He was the last person I would have guessed would be involved in youth ministry. Yet the kids poured in and out of his house and listened to him by the hour. He'd give them advice. They'd talk about premarital sex. "I think it's wrong. It's dead wrong." Then he'd add, "Here's what the Bible says ... " Without using any cute tricks or special gimmicks, he was the finest youth minister we had in our church. Years later, the kids still remembered Ken and those meaningful times. This guy, who cared about kids and who wanted God's word to be known in their midst, was there with them.

Discover the multi-generational gifted people who sit out there. Watch for those people in your church who have those special gifts to work with kids. Let God surprise you.

6. Youth ministry is best led by:

Someone once told me, "Youth ministry is basically done by youth 'coolies'—young adults hired by congregations to work for 20 hours; they're paid for 10; and expected to work 40." The history of those youth "coolies" in a congregation is burnout. Nine months is their average time. And it's no wonder. We take people with great enthusiasm and spirit—but with little experience and skill—and feed them to the lions!

Hosts of competent people run the other direction when we mention youth ministry. "I don't know how to do it," they say. Youth ministry is one of the most difficult ministries in the church. Yet it can be learned. Youth ministry isn't a beginner's job. It's a job that can be developed and built over a lifetime.

7. The following statement best describes the role of young people in my church:

Kid-led ministries rarely last for long. Because the teenage years are a transitional period of time, youth ministry is best done by both youth and adults. One church had 37 adults who committed themselves to youth ministry. Their task: Develop relationships with several kids and "shepherd" them. For a teenager, the "church" is a relationship with another person. Kids need to see the light of Christ in the life of someone they respect.

Youth ministry means adults and youth sharing responsibilities and faith-journeys. Sharing lives is the best gift a congregation can give to young people. And relationships can't be programmed.

Our Lord didn't have many programs. He went about preaching and encountering people; his ministry was people-fed. Jesus communicated God's love. When he left people behind, something had happened to them. Youth ministry happens when we help kids develop a relationship with Christ, with one another and with adults.

A prominent researcher
and seminary professor
tells what it takes to be a
truly effective youth
worker.

CHAPTER 4

Do Kids Count In Your Church?

BY ROLAND MARTINSON

I don't need to tell you that kids count. You know they count because they make a crucial contribution to our contemporary culture. Their energy, ideas, enthusiasm and capacity to ask questions often become the engines of change in the culture around us.

Kids count too because they are a part of today's crucible that shapes and refines the future. Their identity being shaped today is a large part of what the world will look like tomorrow. Their values and lifestyles are an anticipation of the future being born among us.

Kids count. But often they don't count in the church. They aren't taken seriously. For example, you'll find few of the questions of today's youth ever addressed in most pastors' sermons. Secondly, the youth illustrations those pastors use frequently only cite the problems young people experience.

WHERE ARE THE YOUTH IN THE CHURCH?

I often travel and spend time among many congregations of different denominations. I've observed that most worship experiences, the central event of the life of a congregation, are attended by people between the ages of 35 and 55. I rarely see youth. We often fail to take young people seriously in the church. They are rarely allowed the same rights and privileges as other church members. I don't find them having strategic positions in most of our congregations. Young people don't count because they're not enfranchised in the strategic structures of the body of Christ.

Young people have few votes. Their programs have the lowest budgets and they have the least opportunity to speak about their own programs. Kids also often don't count in the church because we don't speak a language that they can understand.

When I was a pastor, I conducted a confirmation class (a process in which we indoctrinate kids during the time they sometimes don't want to hear anything from their adult superiors). I asked my students to take sermon notes. That is, they listened to the Sunday morning sermons and then at class on Wednesdays they handed back some of what they had heard. Tim came one Wednesday with a long face. He looked at me and handed his paper across as if he were really doing so under protest. Then he said: "Let me tell you something. You get up on Sunday morning and you hand out all those empty outlines and on Wednesday I hand back a few notes and nothing important ever passes between us." Fourteen years old and very perceptive.

I perceive that young people often don't count in the church because we are not willing to take seriously the images and language that connect with the world in which they move.

YOUTH HAVE NEGATIVE VIEW OF THE CLERGY

Many young people seem to have acquired an uncomplimentary image of the clergy. I was spending my noon hour in a high school cafeteria, as usual. I'd been asked to give a lecture in a class about marriage and family. A student came up to me and said, "You know, I've had a tough time figuring you out."

"How's that?" I replied. "I'm a pretty simple guy."

"You really sure that you're a pastor?"

"I can show you my clergy card."

She continued: "You sure don't talk like one and you sure

don't act like one. Are you sure you're a minister?"

I asked her how she perceived ministers. She essentially described the clergy as the quintessence of nonsense dressed up in long black robes.

Many young people have left the church. Not only with their bodies, not only with their commitments, but also with their evaluations of who we are as representatives of God's people.

OUR WONDERFUL CHALLENGE

We face a marvelously exciting but crucial challenge. We are those people in the church who rigorously and deeply yearn, wonder, struggle and celebrate about kids, those marvelous persons of God. These young persons—created in the love of God's heart, the wisdom of God's mind, the intuition of God's creativity—can be a part of the organism we call the body of Christ. I'd like to suggest that facilitating this requires courage, creativity and excellence focused on the following four items:

Focus 1: Overcome church inertia. The first focus is to overcome the inertia of the bodies of Christ in which you and I work. To overcome this inertia, we first need to learn about kids and interpret who they are to the larger body of people who don't understand them. The majority of the denominational executives with whom I work do not really know young people anymore. As we look at overcoming that inertia, we need to become advocates of kids' identity among our church colleagues.

We also need to provide support for one another. We need to look into each others' faces to see that we're alive, though perhaps covered with scars, and to have the support of just being together. I think we need to have that flow all the way down through the church so that all those persons who are working with youth have some sort of support for that process. This needs to include the young people.

Focus 2: Know the youth culture. We should help adults listen to kids, learn about them and come to know their culture. Here are ideas on learning about the youth culture:

● Study adolescent psychology. A great deal of marvelous material is available.

● We need to focus on the sociology of the youth culture itself to know its symbols and questions, to look at its affirmations and to read its agenda.

● We need to listen, listen, listen and hear below the words. For instance, people are debating whether a teenage girl who is considering becoming sexually active ought to be able to get birth control devices without parental permission. The debate is raging. Many folks who look at teenage pregnancy and teenage sexual activity across our culture say we need more sex education. How wrong they are. Kids tell me that they do know enough about the facts of sexual activity. Sex education is important, but their sexual activity is a symbol of something far broader and deeper. We must relate on a level where the kids are searching for a deep relationship level, a search for intimacy.

Focus 3: The gospel—legitimate answers. We need to focus on a gospel-based world view and articulation of our message. Kids tell me they often hear messages from the church that don't mean anything to them and in a language they can't understand. They don't hear the church address their real questions. We need to ask: What are the questions kids are raising? What are their assumptions? What are their affirmations? Do they have a part in the sermons?

What are kids' questions? I would like to suggest these: "Am I worth anything? In a world that's competitive, comparing and cutting, is my life worth something? With zits and acne all over my face, am I still valuable? I'm no No. 1, I'm only No. 23. Is it still okay to be me? Do I belong?"

Focus 4: Speak the kid's language. I'd like to suggest that excellence in youth work is the business of enabling the gospel to speak in their language. That's what Jesus did in his parables. That's what Paul did as he carried the gospel into new soil as a missionary. You and I are called to speak clearly so that kids can understand the message and act upon it.

We're also called to develop delivery systems that take seriously that kids live in the fast lane of life. They get up early in the morning and are off to school. I haul my high-school-age daughter to a musical rehearsal at 6:45 in the morning. Then it's on to school. When her classes are finished, she has extracurricular activities. Then it's over to McDonald's to work and then time with her friends. Finally, she changes clothes and plops into bed late at night. It's like that day after day. And you wonder how to do youth programming when life is one mad dash from dawn to dusk.

How do you do programming when the mental capacity to pick up reality has been shaped by a media that turns almost all of knowing into experiential connecting. Kids today learn through the media. They absorb it through their pores, ears and eyes, and they can pick it up from 20 sources at once.

We need to adapt our delivery systems to their culture. We need to know how kids learn and connect. We also need to be able to understand their whole quest for spiritual centering. In attempting to deliver, we often think we have to entice them to come. And so we spend our time dealing with recreation and never get to the questions of: "If God's not up there, if God has no place to be, tell me where is God?"

Or, "I haven't felt God for the last year, and you told me that if I could feel God then I would know he exists. I haven't felt him. Tell me, where is he?"

Or, "I've reasoned to the end of my wits. My 3-year-old brother was killed in a car accident. Tell me about the God who loves. I just stood at my brother's coffin. Tell me about your God."

Our delivery systems need to pick them up at those haunting questions.

The delivery system has to somehow get to the point that we are willing to let down guards, to relate one-to-one and to be unafraid to let the agendas of youth take precedence. When I was in the parish, I knew that my youth ministry had become real when I couldn't carry on ministry in my agenda time and instead had to carry on youth ministry to *their agendas.* When they called and said they needed me. When they knocked on my windows at 11 p.m. and said, "We trust you, we gotta talk."

KIDS COUNT

Kids invigorate me. They sometimes exasperate me. But I see in them a crucible not only of their own future but largely of mine as well. And they count. But often in the church they don't. You and I are called to be students, prophets, priests and evangelists so that the church too can be a place where kids count.

A youth worker entering an established group can take several steps to make the transition as smooth as possible.

Build Trust With Your New Youth Group

BY THOM SCHULTZ

I once received a lengthy letter from a priest who had just moved to a new church and found himself in charge of the youth group. Let me share with you parts of his letter:

"The present situation is this: Not only have I been assigned to take the place of the last priest in this parish, but the youth director has been changed as well. As we both expected, there has been a certain degree of resentment on the part of youth to this new situation. There has been a great deal of 'established procedure' that worked well with the last director. Our 'new direction' is not infrequently met with bitterness, hard feelings, etc. . . . We are told that there are never any adult chaperons present at hayrides . . . .

"There is almost an anti-religious attitude throughout most of the youth. They organize their own weekend retreat once a year, which, I am told, is very well-attended. However, we're told it has been not much more than a weekend camping trip with a closing mass tagged on . . . . We passed out a youth survey last week. Across the board there was the strong desire for the purely social activities with themselves, but an equally strong 'no' for things of social involvement in the community or religious concerns . . . .

"Somehow, I feel the former staff may have been part of the problem, directing themselves only toward the 'good times' that can be had. I've no problem with this in itself, but it appears to be only one very small part of life."

This youth worker is not alone. Various studies show that youth groups keep the same sponsor for an average of only a year.

How should a youth worker approach a new group? The writer of the letter has already made a few blunders.

I'm reminded of another youth leader who moved to Colorado a few years ago. In less than a week, he began announcing some new "guidelines" for the youth group—rules he had used at his former church. The young people hadn't yet healed from the pain of losing their last youth director—and then along came this unfamiliar "impostor," making rules. All but one or two kids left the group—never to return.

A leader entering a new group—especially when he or she follows a strong former leader—should assume a low profile. Listen a lot. Let the members tell you about their group, what it has been doing, what its direction has been. Not only will this process build trust between you and the members, but it affords you the opportunity to gain a picture of the group before your entrance on the scene. A new leader's attempt at sweeping innovations at this time will likely be met with rejection. Get to know everyone first, build trust, then innovate.

Notice I suggested you ask the members themselves about their group. Here we come upon another blunder by the letter writer. He committed a youth ministry "crime" by collecting bits of gossip about his new group from the congregation. Gossip is almost always just that—gossip. Don't solicit it. Don't listen to it. Learn about your new group from the people who *know*.

The writer's survey results are interesting—but not uncommon. Many young people have found religion unfashionable. Building an appreciation for God and service to others is a process. It is not something that snaps into place because the youth worker says it should. Successful youth leaders have seen their young people's spiritual interests begin to awaken naturally after the leaders and members have built a bond of trust—and the members become genuinely curious about the leaders' spiritual life. That trust is often developed through a lot of "good times" or "social activities."

A young person who *asks* about God is on his way to a stronger faith than a kid who is force-fed "God talk."

ADDITIONAL READING

Encyclopedia of Serendipity, Lyman Coleman, Serendipity House.

Getting Together: A Guide for Good Groups, Em Griffin, InterVarsity.

Starting a Youth Ministry, Larry Keefauver, Group Books.

Are you the flashiest person in your group? Or are you super straight? Whatever your style, do this self-inventory to discover how you really relate with young people.

Evaluate How You Relate To Young People

BY MARGARET RICKERS

"I need to talk to somebody I can trust," Jim confided to his friend Tom. "I mean, I know I can trust you, Tom, but I really need the ideas of someone older—someone who has some experience."

Tom hesitated because Jim didn't attend his church. But he suggested: "Why don't you talk to the youth minister at my church? She's really nice and knows how to listen without telling you you're doing everything wrong. She never makes you feel dumb or anything like that. I'm sure she'd be willing to help you. Her name is Alice."

Jim thought a moment, then replied: "That's funny—I don't even know the last name of my church's youth director. Everyone just calls him 'Buddy.' I've tried to talk to him—once—but he didn't seem interested. He just tried to be cool and act like he was a teenager. It really turned me off. I never even think of talking to him."

That conversation might reflect people you know. Successful youth ministry means more than throwing adults together with teenagers or giving someone the title of youth director.

Youth ministry involves relationships. Relating to young people implies a variety of factors that enter the youth/adult picture. And you, as a youth leader, may not even be aware of all the components affecting your relationships with young people.

The following inventory is designed to help you discover more about yourself. As you check where you fit, rate your relationships with the young people. Remember, the inventory illustrates extremes; so it might not describe you *exactly*, but it will provide a range or responses that could suggest your particular ministry-style. Be honest. Be prepared to grow. See areas where you need improvement and learn where you can use your positive qualities to help others.

Language

I know all the youth jargon and speak it fluently and often.	I try to speak youth jargon, but don't succeed in communicating with it.	I know youth jargon, but don't try to use it.	I don't pay any attention to the language and vocabulary of teenagers.

Music

I could list the "Top 10" on the record chart this week—or any other week.	I follow the top rock music and even have a poster of a popular recording artist on my office door.	I am familiar with some of the more popular groups; I listen to that music if the kids want to and if the music is appropriate.	I will not listen to the kids' music nor let them listen to it in my presence.

Dress

Anyone who saw me walking down the street would think I am a teenager by the way I dress.	I know what's "in" and compliment the young people who wear those things well.	I haven't even noticed what's "in" these days.	I think the way kids dress today is disgusting.

Attitute Toward Sexual Values

The kids will do what they want, so I don't discuss sex with them.	I think teenagers are afraid to talk to me or other adults about sex.	We teach a sex education class and have good discussions on the subject.	I lecture the kids all the time admonishing them to not have sexual relationships.

Confidentiality

I'd never tell anyone what young people say; I don't want to lose the kids' friendship.	I carefully weigh what I'm told and then decide whether it's necessary to tell someone else.	I feel compelled to tell parents or friends whatever kids tell me.	It doesn't make any difference if I tell someone what the kids say—they're just talking.

Being Me

The kids consider me one of them.	The young people see me as I am—usually at my best, but sometimes at my worst.	I put on my best behavior whenever I'm with the kids, so they'll be impressed.	Teenagers see me as a "super-Christian" and keep me on a pedestal.

Faith Sharing

If they didn't know I work at a church, they probably wouldn't know I believe in God.	I show my faith and express it in my language and my life.	I'm always reminding kids to act like Christians.	My Bible classes and youth meetings all sound like sermons.

My Lifestyle

I'm always at the kids' favorite hangouts and anywhere else kids go.	I support young people by showing an interest in what they do, attending games and concerts, and occasionally visiting their favorite hangouts.	I think kids should know I'm available; I encourage them to make appointments with me at church.	I'm too busy with other things to spend any extra time with teenagers.

How did you rate? Are you stuck in one extreme? What did you discover about how you relate to young people? Do you feel comfortable with your ministry-style? What would you like to change about yourself?

Twenty-five youth group members were asked to evaluate the inventory categories. Comments included:

Language. "What do you mean 'youth jargon'? Most of us don't talk any differently from you." The media often concentrate on reporting the language and culture of a small minority of kids who are grabbing attention.

Music. "I know everyone has different tastes. If my folks liked the kind of music I like, I'd probably change—just to be different. But if they tell me I can't listen to what I want to hear, then I get mad. I know some of it's trash, but it doesn't mean I believe it just because I listen to it. I like the beat and the feeling it gives me. That's why I really like Christian rock too."

Dress. "I like it when our youth director comments on my clothes. I think I have good taste and I try to be in style. But if our youth director wore today's styles at her age, she'd look like a fool—and I wouldn't want to be seen with her."

Attitude toward sexual values. "We have really good sex education classes in school and at church. I'm sure I probably know more about the subject than my parents knew when they got married; in fact, that's what they tell me. There's nothing worse than an adult who refuses to talk about sex or gets embarrassed when the subject comes up. That's life! We don't need a lecture every time the word is mentioned; we know what it's about."

Confidentiality. "If I tell our youth director something, I expect him to keep it a secret unless I say it's okay to tell someone else. He needs to ask my permission if he's considering talking to my parents about it. And then he'd need to tell my why."

Being me. "Sometimes I get the feeling my parents are trying to be perfect in raising me and they seem super-human. I want them to be real. That goes for our pastor and our youth director too."

Faith sharing. "You can tell if someone's a Christian by the way he acts. We don't need to hear sermons every day of the week or every time we come to church. But I do expect our youth leader to act like a Christian."

My lifestyle. "It made me feel really good when our youth director came to our school choir's musical. My folks liked it too. But it sure would be a drag if he showed up every place I was. I'd feel like he was checking on me or something. Sometimes I just need to be alone with my friends—even my church friends."

SUGGESTIONS FOR FUTURE RELATING

Consider the following tips to enhance your relationships with young people:

1. Youth leaders are most respected when they're themselves. Trying to dress or talk like a teenager doesn't enhance "image" or add to the relationship.

2. Judgmental attitudes toward dress, friends, language or music don't build positive relationships. Take time to find out and understand why young people are "into" the things that are part of their lives.

3. Trust enters into almost every area of relationships. Keep your trust level and your credibility high with teenagers. Always ask permission before you betray a confidence—even in cases where you're legally bound to tell. Chances are you can get permission before you share the secret.

4. Reflect your faith in your life and relationships. Don't

be a preacher of the Good News by ramming it down kids' throats. Be a sharer of God's wonderous love in all you do.

5. Show care and concern for everyone. Be fair in your dealings with young people. Don't play favorites. Be honest. But most of all—be yourself!

Happy relating!

ADDITIONAL READING

Counseling Teenagers, G. Keith Olson, Group Books.

Peoplemaking, Virginia Satir, Science and Behavior Books.

Please Understand Me: Character and Temperament Types, David Keirsey and Marilyn Bates, Prometheus Nemesis Books.

Listening, a primary means
of communication, is
crucial for your ministry
with youth.

CHAPTER
7

Show You Care: Develop Your Listening Skills

BY ROLAND LARSON

Have you ever tried to say something and it seemed that nobody listened? Or you were relating an incident when someone interrupted and changed the subject? That probably left you feeling put down, ignored and angry. Some corporations budget millions of dollars annually to teach their employees how to listen. Business executives, managers, supervisors and clerical workers are discovering how important it is to listen. Why? Because in the long run effective listening saves money, time and human energy. It cuts down on mistakes. Good listening helps a corporation run more smoothly and increases the effectiveness of everyday interaction and teamwork. Considerable pain and stress are removed when persons care enough to hear each other, and try to understand and respond with genuine concern.

Listening, the primary communication skill, is crucial for us to work effectively with youth. It can work wonders in relationships that are being built or in ones that need to be rebuilt.

Let's acknowledge from the start that you can't *always* listen. There are times when you need to confront the other person and let him or her know clearly and honestly what you are experiencing at that time. More about that later.

A LISTENING ATTITUDE

Effective listening requires listening knowledge and skills, but an important beginning point is your listening attitude. With a healthy attitude, the listener says to himself or herself: "Joe is an important person. He has something worthwhile and important to say. I can probably learn from Joe. I'm going to try right now to understand what he is saying and feeling. I may have to slow down my own reactions; I'm going to listen whether I agree with him or not."

LISTENING TO REMEMBER SOMEONE'S NAME

There are various levels or kinds of listening. At different times and in different situations, we listen for different things. For example, sometimes we listen carefully to a new acquaintance's name to catch it and remember it so we can call that person by name in the future. It's an important listening skill in effective human relationships. But I constantly hear people say, "I can't remember names."

If you want to remember someone's name, you can do it with this simple skill: First, focus on the other person and *observe* everything you can about him or her. Second, *associate* his or her name with a story or a situation and get a mental picture of it. (Sometimes the crazier the association, the better.) Third, *repeat* the person's name in your mind until you have it. This might take a bit of practice, but you'll find that you are listening to names in a way that helps your computer-like brain recall them. Each of us likes to be called by name. It's an important dimension of listening in youth-adult relationships. Try observation, association and repetition.

LISTENING FOR INFORMATION

Sometimes our purpose in listening is to gather data or information about something or someone. At other times, we listen to someone's instructions as we work together on a task. In these situations it is helpful to clarify by asking questions and listening to the other's responses. If the matter isn't clear, keep questioning and discussing until you understand what the other person is saying. You might need to restate or paraphrase the other person's statement ("What I hear you saying is . . ." or something similar). Such checking back helps you know that you've heard accurately. That's part of concerned listening!

LISTENING FOR DEEPER MEANINGS

The heart of effective listening in working with youth is listening for deeper meanings—the message behind the words. An opportunity to listen is at hand when a young person, or anyone for that matter, comes to you with a concern or problem and needs to talk. At this time the attitudes, knowledge and skills for listening are particularly crucial. To be a helping person in this situation means that you listen instead of talk, even if you have a problem at the same moment as the other person. This is your real chance to give the gift of listening.

The challenge is to put aside your own concerns and focus on the other person. A person who had begun doing this, a participant in one of my listening workshops, told me, "During the last four weeks, I've learned more about my teenage son than I learned in the previous 15 years." Dad had changed his listening style.

How does listening or not listening work in a real life situation? Think about the following interchange to examine some helpful and not-so-helpful ways of responding to a young person who comes to you with a problem. Lori seeks you out when you are alone and says: "You wouldn't believe what a rotten day I had at school today. Everything seemed to go wrong—that place stinks. I studied hard for the test today and this teacher switched the rules and tested us on stuff he must have covered last Wednesday, the only day of school I've missed all year! I'm so fed up I'd just as soon drop out of school."

Lori pauses. What do you say? Here are responses by four adults.

Adult No. 1: "I don't blame you for being upset, but that's the way it is in lots of real life situations. I know just how you feel. Last month I thought everything was falling apart in my office. Just when I had my final report ready for my boss, he switched the rules on me too. Here's what happened to me . . ."

10 Commandments for Good Listening

1. Stop talking! You cannot listen if you are talking. Polonius in Shakespeare's **Hamlet** said it well, "Give every man thine ear, but few thy voices."

2. Put the talker at ease. Help the speaker feel that he is free to talk. This is often called a "permissive environment."

3. Show him that you want to listen. Look and act interested. Do not read your mail while the person talks. Listen to understand rather than compete to reply.

4. Remove distractions. Don't doodle, tap or shuffle papers. Will it be quieter if the door is closed?

5. Empathize. Try to put yourself in the speaker's place so that you can see his or her point of view.

6. Be patient. Allow plenty of time. Do not interrupt. Don't start for the door or walk away.

7. Hold your temper. An angry person gets the wrong meaning from words.

8. Go easy on argument and criticism. This puts the other person on the defensive. The speaker may "clam up" or get angry. Do not argue: Even if you win, you lose.

9. Ask clarifying questions. This encourages the speaker and shows you are listening. It helps to further develop points.

10. Stop talking! This is first and last, because all other commandments depend on it. You just can't do a good listening job while you are talking.

God gave man two ears but only one tongue, which is a gentle hint that we should listen more than talk.

Adult No. 2: "Come on, don't let it get you down. You've probably got enough decent grades in the past to pull you through. If not, you can take charge of the situation for the rest of the year and get your grade up. Don't let situations like that get the best of you. You've got to appreciate that every one of these teachers at your school probably has your best interests at heart."

Adult No. 3: "How come you signed up for that math course anyway? I remember once before you told me how hard math was for you." (Pause—adult walks over to the small stack of today's mail.) "I'm looking for that pair of tickets for tomorrow night's ball game at the stadium. My friend and I are going—should be a good game. Oh, what did this teacher do that bugged you so much?"

Adult No. 4: "Sounds like you really had a rough day. Care to tell me more about it?"

If you were the young person with a need to talk about your problem, which response would be most helpful to you? Which would be least helpful? Rank them from 1 to 4; 1 the best approach, 4 the worst.

Here's what happens in each response:

Adult No. 1: Shifts the focus to self rather than really recognizing that Lori needs to deal with her own problem. Seems sympathetic but is giving reassurance that distracts from what Lori wants to talk about. He or she is an ineffective listener—blowing it when there's a chance to listen. The listening style is more like "I can top that!"

Adult No. 2: Like Adult No. 1, Adult No. 2's intentions are good, but he or she is doing a poor job when there's a chance to listen. Talks a lot and likes to tell others what to do. Is quite expert at giving advice when Lori hasn't even asked for it. A great moralizer, usually a judgmental person, often characterized by interrupting the other person with "Yes, but . . ."

Adult No. 3: Gives the impression of not being interested, distracting Lori's train of thought and apparently ignoring the fact that Lori has a deep concern. Loses eye contact by stepping away. Thinks he or she is listening, but Lori is convinced he or she isn't. This person's diverting tactics come across as non-caring. This person is "listening with a half ear" (maybe less).

Adult No. 4: Is immediately focusing on Lori and tuning in to her feelings. Has begun a listening process, demonstrating an interest in what Lori is saying and feeling. This adult is a listener who recognizes Lori's need to talk and provides that opportunity for her. This adult will continue to focus on Lori right now, putting aside his or her own needs in order to listen to Lori and try to understand what she is experiencing. That's "listening with the heart."

Adult No. 4 is on the way to opening communication with Lori by drawing her out and inviting her to talk—and then being a sensitive and interested listener. He or she will do this by:

- focusing on what Lori is saying
- being responsive to Lori's feelings
- having eye-to-eye contact (but not a staring contest)
- not dominating the interaction
- not judging, moralizing or lecturing

- giving little or no advice (unless asked for, and then cautiously)
- showing acceptance and understanding
- responding with an occasional nod, smile, etc.
- watching and listening for non-verbal communication—tone of voice, increase in volume, facial expression and body language (80 to 90 percent of the message is non-verbal).

CARING, NOT CURING

While conducting hundreds of listening workshops around the world, I've repeatedly noticed a communications pattern which interferes with many persons' ability to listen effectively. When someone presents a problem, the would-be listener listens for a while and then jumps in, attempting to solve the other's problem—often before the person speaking has had a chance to spell out his or her feelings and concerns. Sometimes we mistakenly think we must "cure" the person—to diagnose his or her situation and give some kind of solution. But what we need is an attitude of caring rather than curing.

DIFFICULT SITUATIONS

There may be times when the other person's behavior really bothers you, and you find it inappropriate or impossible to listen. For example, the other person wastes your energy and good will by repeatedly talking about the same thing. That's frustrating for you. Try saying something like, "Jill, we've gone over this same situation together several times in the last few weeks, and I need to know if there's some new part or another dimension of it that you want to talk about today."

At times other conditions may make it difficult for you to listen. For example, you don't have the time; you are on your way to a meeting. Say, "Tim, I'm really interested in what you're saying, but I'm due at a meeting downstairs in five minutes. Can we set a time to continue talking about this later?" Establishing a linkage for future contact assures the other person that you have begun to hear the message and that you are interested.

LEADERSHIP CHALLENGE

Your job of listening is seemingly endless. Young people

often are burdened by the many concerns of growing up in today's world, and many are particularly burdened by the expectations of those around them. You cannot expect to help solve all of their problems. But you can be alongside them as a loving, caring listener. Just listening to youth non-judgmentally goes a long way. And if you run into a serious problem, refer your friend to a trusted professional person.

While the cost of not listening to youth cannot be measured in dollars, it can be seen in incomplete or thwarted relationships. It has been demonstrated time and again that the effective listener is a more effective leader. You can be that type of listener.

WHEN YOU LISTEN . . .

1. Do you show an interest in learning about other persons, places and things?

2. Do you try to put yourself in the other person's shoes?

3. Do you tune in on a person's feelings as well as the words being spoken?

4. Do you try to overcome your own emotional attitudes, responses and prejudgments?

5. Do you try to understand the main ideas, attitudes and feelings being communicated?

6. Do you avoid interrupting? Especially, do you curb the impulse to cut in and complete the other person's sentences?

7. Do you ever ask for feedback on how people rate you as a listener?

8. Do you consciously practice listening skills?

9. Do you listen to others as you would like for them to listen to you?

ADDITIONAL READING

The Caring Question, Donald A. Tubesing and Nancy Loving Tubesing, Augsburg.

Friend to Friend, J. David Stone and Larry Keefauver, Group Books.

The Skilled Helper: A Model for Systematic Helping and Interpersonal Relating, Gerard Egan, Brooks-Cole.

Do the problems your
young people tell you keep
you awake at night? When
do you keep secrets and
when do you tell?

CHAPTER
8

What to Tell
Or Not Tell:
Confidentiality

BY JOANI SCHULTZ

"I' m telling you this," begins Scott, "because you're
the only person I can trust, and I know you won't
say anything."

You summon all your listening skills.

"You know I really love Laura, and we've even talked
about getting married someday. Well, uh, we've gotten
pretty involved and . . . ."

There's a painful pause.

"I think Laura's pregnant."

You hide your surprise.

"Our folks would kill us if they knew we were having
sex . . . so Laura and I have decided she's getting an
abortion."

A strange and sickening sensation strikes. The news tears
your heart apart. As Scott's youth leader and friend, you
wonder: Shouldn't his parents know about this?

Along with the problem of telling parents comes a painful
realization. As a trusted confidant, not only do you hear the
"good stuff" from kids, you also become aware of hurtful

and difficult issues they're facing. That paradox turns ministry dreams into nightmares. Scott and Laura's situation is
only one example. There are other common youth ministry
confidentiality issues.

What do you do when youth group members divulge information about their parents—that their parents wouldn't
want you to know? Because of that information, you struggle
with your responsibility of stepping in or staying out. For instance, Sally comes to the youth group with a badly bruised
arm and a cut under her eye. In a burst of emotion, she describes what happened when her father beat her. Between
uncontrollable sobs, Sally adds, "Dad would really hurt me
if he knew I told."

Your role as youth leader poses other problems. For example, is it best to keep parents sheltered from their teenager's dishonesty? Or will disclosing the "bad stuff" be the
most loving thing to do?

What would you do in this situation: Stan's parents drop
him off each week at the church so he can attend the youth
group. He waits until they leave and then slips downtown.
When the youth meeting is over, Stan conveniently appears
at the church. His parents think he's been there all the time.
You discover Stan's tactics, confront him, and wonder if you
should tell his parents.

What happens when young people need loving confrontation concerning their behavior—but their parents hold pres-
tigious positions in the community or congregation? Telling
prominent parents news that reflects their tainted teenager—or worse yet, not-so-perfect parents—could jeopardize
your ministry. For example, consider this all-too-true problem: Lately you've become more aware of Sherri's loose behavior. "I really like guys," she snips, "and I don't think
there's anything wrong in letting them know that!" Your uneasiness grows because she doesn't hide any details of her
sexual escapades. For you, the problem is compounded by
the fact that her father is the president of your congregation.

When is it appropriate to inform parents of their teenager's involvement in something illegal? Offenses against the
law muddy the confidentiality issue even more. What is your
responsibility to the young person, the parents and the law,
when your information involves legal matters? What should

you do, for example, if you catch two kids smoking pot during a retreat? All the group members know about the incident and you deal with it during the retreat. Now you wonder—is this something their parents should know too?

These encounters aren't unusual for most of us to experience. Our role as youth leaders invites situations and conversations that sometimes the parents should know. That's why it is a challenge to approach each situation creatively and carefully. Learning why confidentiality is a problem and discovering how to meet the challenge is the next step in unfolding workable answers.

WHY CONFIDENTIALITY IS A PROBLEM

To-tell-or-not-to-tell encounters happen because you're someone kids will seek out. Adolescence Journal studied adolescents' perception of significant adults. The amazing discovery: Ministers and youth ministers were sought out, second only to parents! When teenagers seek guidance and information, they will turn to people like you. Consider yourself a significant, approachable adult in the eyes of young people.

PREVENTING THE PROBLEM

Remember: Never underestimate your significance in the lives of young people. Don't be surprised when you're approached with heavy information. Knowing you'll be involved in confidential sharing provides an awareness basis. With that in mind, prevent sticky situations by avoiding promises that can't be kept.

Dr. C. Keith Olson, author of **Counseling Teenagers,** warns, "Remember the most important thing: Never get backed into a corner by promising confidentiality *before* you know the information. This way you avoid being trapped in a no-win situation." Olson's words offer wise preventative measures for your protection. How often has someone bargained, "I want to tell you something, but you've got to promise not to tell anyone"? Caution lights flash. Because you care, you know keeping information private isn't always an act of love.

If you're feeling manipulated, remind your friend: "I'm here for your good and benefit. Trust I will do the best on your behalf." Then talk about trust. If that's too frightening, allow the freedom for him or her to back away. It's important to provide the choice of not divulging information. If the young person doesn't share, follow up with a call or visit.

Often a young person who risks information is actually reaching out for help. One youth worker shared this incident: Plopping down in her office one day, a youth group member proceeded to roll a marijuana cigarette and ask, "You want to learn how to roll a joint?" The leader was taken aback but realized there was more behind this action than a question. The conversation led to intense sharing of that young person's struggles. The trusted relationship with the youth leader led to personal growth and change for that young person. Revealing information takes many forms, but ultimately means, "I want help."

TO TELL OR NOT TO TELL—HOW TO DECIDE

What do you do when you're trapped between ministering to kids and being a good steward of information to parents? The solution is learning to raise and answer certain critical questions. By carefully weighing all the issues, using common sense and prayer, you can make good decisions.

Step 1: Gather Accurate Information

First, make certain you're working with correct data. Remember Scott and his pregnant girlfriend, Laura? Let's work through that problem.

Get the facts by asking questions. Is Laura really pregnant? Will their parents really disown them or react irrationally? Is Laura planning an abortion? Help Scott and Laura sort through their feelings and hold to the facts. Be ready to deal with deeper issues that might be uncovered by the process.

Step 2: What Would Happen If . . .

Next trace through what would happen if the parents knew and what would happen if they didn't know. Draw two columns. Label one "tell" and the other "don't tell." Fill in each column by writing consequences and speculations. Ask as many questions as you can. Here are some question examples:

● Why hasn't the young person told his or her parents?

● Where might the continuing behavior of the young person lead?

● Would the family relationships suffer or grow if the parents are told?

● Is it necessary for the parents to know?

● How would things be different if the parents knew?

● How would my relationship with the parents and young person change if I tell?

● What is in the best interest of the young person?

● What is in the best interest of the parents?

● Is anyone in danger or in a life-threatening situation?

Step 3: Weigh the Alternatives

Remember, telling a parent is more than a revelation of knowledge. You must identify a goal, a purpose, a caring cause and a reason for doing so. This becomes clear by looking at the "what ifs."

With Scott and Laura, you could ask if it is necessary for them to tell their parents. Do you feel strongly that telling their parents is needed? Would the relationships suffer or grow if the parents knew? Would Laura and Scott be denied to see each other again? Would parents accuse or place blame? Will they rise to the occasion and join in on a decision that's best for everyone? Is it important that Laura not get an abortion if she's pregnant?

THREE WAYS TO TELL PARENTS

If you're convinced that it's necessary for the parents to know certain information, decide how you will inform them. Here are three ways to let parents know. Each has its own benefits and difficulties.

The young person tells the parents. Ask questions. Would this method of sharing encourage or discourage communication? With no intervention, could the situation become violent or explosive? Do you think the young person would really follow through? For example, Scott and Laura probably wouldn't have the courage to face their parents.

You tell the parents. In almost every situation, when trust has been established between young people and their leader, the leader consults with them first. As a leader, share your concerns and allow the young person to be a part of the decision-making process. Here are questions you could ask yourself:

● Would it appear as though I'm butting in?

● Would my presence help make peace or create tension?

● Would talking without the young person foster more open and honest communication between parents?

● What would be the benefit of bringing this information to the parents by myself?

You and the young person tell the parents. By going with the young person, you provide support and become a liaison. Before you talk with the parents, clarify your goals with the young person. Discuss the reasons for both of you being there. Don't take sides or gang up on the parents. Agree ahead of time on what is to be your role. Is it to clarify, to listen, to articulate the problem or concern, or to present the case? Will your presence clarify misunderstandings or will you pose a threat?

SPEAKING OUT

We asked young people to respond to this question, "When you speak with your youth leader, do you expect him or her to keep what you say a secret?"

Here's what four youth group members had to say:

"If I tell my leader something personal, I expect him to ask my permission to talk about it to other people. If what I say isn't important, I wouldn't mind as much."

Doug Heitz

"I don't expect my leader to do anything, because I know she won't tell anybody anything unless I say it's okay to. I can always count on her to be there just to listen."

Julie Knudson

"Keeping what you say confidential is important, but it can be taken too far. If someone tells a leader that he's going to commit suicide, the leader should tell someone else. In general, though, secrecy is important."

Peter Franck

"I expect my leader to keep what I tell her a secret, especially from my parents. Not that I'm doing anything wrong, there are just things I want to discuss with my leader and no one else."

Diana Henkens

How to Be a Friend to a Friend in Crisis

"Most people don't realize how important they can be in helping a friend through a personal crisis," says Rich Van Pelt, a veteran youth worker with troubled adolescents.

Rich offers the following tips to help a friend who is experiencing a crisis. You can genuinely help by being:

● **Compassionate.** The more you care about someone, the more you can help.

● **Accepting.** The person who is facing a crisis needs to feel secure around you.

● **Genuine.** People in crisis situations look for someone who has no particular motives other than helping.

● **Sensitive.** A friend to a friend in crisis knows how to respond emotionally. The sensitive helper also knows which actions and words the person in crisis responds to best.

● **Humorous.** A sense of humor often breaks the tensions that inevitably build.

● **Competent.** While you don't need to be an expert to help a friend, you do need to be aware of ways of responding to your friend's crisis.

Here are some principles for helping a friend.

● **Availability.** There are two kinds of availability: 1.) Actions often communicate louder than words. You can often help by just being there. 2.) You're not helping the person so much through your ability to give expert counseling, but because you care enough to focus your attentions on him or her.

● **Expect you can help.** One of the most helpful tools you have for helping a friend is your relationship with him or her. Trust, openness and concern are just as valuable as formal counseling skills.

● **Empathize with the person.** Work on developing the ability to feel what he or she is experiencing emotionally.

● **Listen carefully.** Practice listening to people and asking follow-up questions to get at what they really mean.

According to Rich, one of the worst dangers is to listen just enough to "counsel" the person.

● **Be willing to talk about anything.** Don't be uncomfortable if your friend wants to talk specifically about the crisis. Be willing to give your friend the emotional freedom to talk about anything he or she wants.

● **Don't judge.** A person in crisis won't be as levelheaded as you'd like him or her to be. Being rational and logical may not help much. Allow the person to express what he or she is feeling without fearing a judgmental response from you.

● **Use spiritual resources.** Use the Bible to comfort and assure the person. Pray with him or her.

● **Be a resource person.** Sometimes you may help most by being a servant—by providing food or transportation, contacting people, making telephone calls and doing "little" things.

The pressure is on. People like to gauge the success of your group by its size. But the "numbers game" is dangerous play.

CHAPTER 9

Small Group Or Big Group: Which Is Better?

BY LEE SPARKS

A church in Winter Park, Florida, draws nearly 1,000 teenagers weekly to its youth program. In the shadow of this giant, a youth pastor in a nearby church said he sometimes feels inadequate. "I feel pressure from within myself to get a bigger and bigger group," he said. "Sometimes I wonder what's wrong with me when I only get 50 or 60 kids when the other church pulls in 1,000." The harried guy also admitted that the church leadership lays covert pressure on him to draw larger numbers. The subtle value: *Bigger is better.*

As a part-time youth director at a church in Oklahoma City, I had a small group with an average attendance of about 12 to 15 (including both junior and senior high). The Christian education committee called a meeting to discuss the youth group. The first issue was size, and I found myself defending the smallness. Eventually, I won the committee over (maybe), but I began to wonder about the value underlying my argument: *Smaller is better.*

Today's church sees a meshing of different group size values. Sometimes a church defines success as a lot of young bodies running around the building. Another church may be perfectly content to have five or six kids regularly meeting in the basement in a room furnished with beat-up couches and an old black-and-white television.

Rich Bimler, executive director of the board for youth services of the Lutheran Church—Missouri Synod, recalls his frustrations as a youth pastor when church leaders focused on numbers. "People would ask me how many I had at meetings instead of what happened at the meeting," he said. "Somebody once said we tend to plan for quality in youth ministry, but we evaluate on quantity."

Is bigger better? Is smaller better? No and no. Both values are secondary to far greater criteria for evaluating what you're doing. Here are some criteria "eggs" to put in your "basket":

BIBLICAL BASIS

Many churches are run by successful business and professional people. Some of their jobs depend on how many pieces they produce or how many accounts they secure. They may expect a similar mode of operation for the church and, in a way, want to run the church as a business. It is at this time that your understanding of the Bible can be helpful.

Jesus had much contact with large crowds. Wherever he ventured around Palestine, a crowd gathered. Some extraordinary things happened with these crowds such as the feedings, ripping off a roof to lower a sick man into a crowded house and speaking from a boat because the crowd had pressed too far toward the waterline. But in the end the crowd turned against him.

The smaller group, however, was the context for many major events in Jesus' ministry. Jesus had a small group of 12, sent out 70 in pairs, appeared to only three at the Transfiguration, conversed with the solitary woman at the well, was crucified with a couple of ruffians, and after his resurrection greeted three women and later the disciples.

Other biblical references are plentiful. Paul had a small group which evangelized to a huge geographical area. Joshua depended on two scouts to assist in conquering

Jericho. The prophets referred time and again to the small remnant of Jews devoted to Yahweh.

Don't misuse the Bible to claim special authority for yourself or your cause since the Bible shows the possibilities of both large and small groups. Simply point out there is biblical room for both.

RELATIONSHIPS

Youth ministry is marked by good relationships. The youth leaders must develop and maintain good relationships with the young people. The leaders also need to share significant time together among themselves. They also need to develop healthy relationships with parents and the church leadership. Crisis situations are easier to deal with if there is good rapport among all the groups affected by youth ministry.

In the group itself, a good size for a quality experience is five to eight, with a maximum of 12. Larger groups can be divided into smaller groups. Young people tend to feel more comfortable in smaller, intimate groups. These groups encourage accceptance and understanding. Each individual has more power than in the spectator-like rally meeting. Large group meetings are not necessarily bad. Sometimes kids need the anonymity of a face in the crowd. However, the person behind the face will usually experience little growth in the crowd.

PERSONAL GROWTH

Youth leaders are in a place where they can see young people grow and mature. Adolescence is a time of frantic development as teenagers search for identity. Few adults other than parents and perhaps school teachers receive the opportunity to gauge an adolescent's growth. The church leadership is often out of touch with individual youth. A good youth leader can help the church leadership get back in touch.

Explain to the church leadership the kind of growth you see happening in young persons' lives. Describe the kinds of quality relationships going on with the youth and leaders.

EFFICIENCY

Efficiency is another term for stewardship. It has to do with how well you set your goals; plan and execute your activities to fulfill those goals; and use your resources of time, money and persons.

Small groups may appear to be more efficient. Five or six can be easily mobilized. Goals and activities are easier to accomplish than with a crowd. But small groups also have some limitations. Smaller groups have fewer resources to fulfill a goal. They can decline into a snobbish clique.

So, the size of a group has less to do with its efficiency than the abilities of leaders to get organized and get going. It is, however, important for a group to identify where it is going and how it's going to get there.

GROUP GROWTH

As your group grows together—building relationships, developing as individuals and fulfilling some of its goals— chances are good for growth in numbers. Perhaps you'll experience explosive growth. If this happens, here are a couple of things to think about:

Increase quality with numbers. Jesus warned about the dangers of unhealthy growth in the Parable of the Seeds. The plants died because of poor roots. As your group grows, root your ministry in spiritual discipline, efficient use of resources and careful delegation of responsibilities.

Freeze your ego. If the youth group is successful, in the sense of the criteria above, God may send the numbers to it. If this happens, avoid the temptation to forget the source of success. Smug, know-it-all youth leaders hurt the ministry. The Bible illustrates the tragedy of leaders who began with humble hearts, experienced success and growth, and then fell into arrogance (remember Samson? David? Judas?). The sign of an experienced leader is humility and gentleness. The experienced leader remembers God, thanking him for success in the group, small or large.

ADDITIONAL READING

Starting a Youth Ministry, Larry Keefauver, Group Books.
Youth Ministries: Thinking Big With Small Groups, Carolyn C. Brown, Abingdon.

The question of who has
control can lead to frus-
tration and tension. There
are positive measures to
take when you and your
group don't agree.

Managing Power Struggles Within Your Group

BY RICH BIMLER

TUCSON, ARIZONA—Youth Director Mark Hayes is "missing in action" and hasn't been seen since last Sunday's youth group meeting when he and the youth group fought over the group's priorities.

BOGOTA, NEW JERSEY—Youth ministers Mr. and Mrs. Sam Winne transferred to another church after telling their young people that the youth group was just one large clique.

BIEGLOW, WYOMING—Associate pastor Melvin Qualm asked for a six-month leave of absence because some of the major needs he felt young people should be discussing weren't the needs the young people cared to discuss.

MISTY RIDGE, OREGON—Lay youth worker Hazel Schwartz insisted that all teenagers in her church enroll in a back-to-the-Bible basic study course. Her concept of God didn't agree with her youth group's concept of God.

Those examples are just four areas in which power struggles can happen between young people and their leaders. Check it out with your own experiences. Think of times when you've felt frustration and tension over the question of "Who's got the power."

Wherever people are together, struggles and tensions are going to develop. It's called human nature. Sin. As we adult leaders seek support, young people too are seeking attention and encouragement. Sometimes the conflicting needs of youth and adults can cause power struggles and create hard feelings and resentment. Rather than blaming one side or the other, we need to try to see these experiences as avenues for ministry.

Power struggles are real. They happen. But there are things you can do to minimize the destruction.

HOW TO AVOID POWER STRUGGLES

Here are 10 "resolves" that some youth groups have developed in the area of power struggles between young people and leaders:

1. Find the real issue. This takes time and honesty. Often only surface feelings arise. ("I'm not going to cooperate with Mr. Harvey because he didn't say 'Hi' to me one Sunday" or, "Since she was late for the meeting, I just won't ask her to do anything anymore.")

2. Set objectives with your youth group. Then stick to those. Look at the young people's needs and decide what your group can and wants to do to respond to those needs.

3. Communicate. Keep in touch verbally and also by newsletter, phone, posters, group meetings, announcements and any other ways that help youth group members and adult leaders know what your youth group is all about. Remember, though, you cannot be "all things to all people."

4. Develop priorities together. Adult leaders should not "lay on" their agendas to the youth groups or youth officers. Work together so that all have a part in deciding on the priorities.

5. Delegate. Use your youth officers or other small groups of young people to outline your youth group schedule. Involve as many young people as possible in developing and communicating your youth group's plans.

6. Build relationships. Work at ways to continue to develop closer relationships with the adults and young people involved in your group. Work diligently at building a caring community by spending more time together, doing more things in small groups, taking trips together, working on specific projects together in small groups and sharing thoughts and feelings.

7. Be broadly based. Deal with as many issues as possible through your youth group. The group can't do it all, but you can be more sensitive in allowing the entire group to have ownership as to what is to be discussed and shared.

8. Keep God in the picture. Continue to see that God is the focal point of all that the youth group does. Assume it. Reaffirm it. Continue to proclaim that God is constantly present with each individual, as well as your group. Thank him for his presence.

9. Work on forgiving. Forgive one another for the past times when power was misused. Forgive and continue to care for those who misunderstood you or were misunderstood by you. Forgiveness is the key to relationships in the Lord!

10. Continue to own the ministry together. It isn't the pastor's ministry; it isn't the youth's ministry. It is the church's ministry—youth and adults together, praising, proclaiming and serving the Lord.

Forget about who has the power and remind each other that the real power for ministry comes from the Spirit, who is alive and well in each of us.

MEETING OUTLINE:
Dealing With Power Struggles in Your Group

Here's a simple process to follow with your group when you sense a power struggle developing. Discuss each of the following items with your group, both leaders and young people, to see how each relates to your situation.

● With your group, attempt to surface some of the tensions. What are some of the struggles you are facing? List them. No need to agree or disagree yet, just get them out for all to see. Your list may include:

____ The youth adviser won't let us do what we want.

____ The youth group doesn't seem to be interested in anything.

Resolving Conflict

Occasionally, everyone experiences conflict—especially in group situations.

Following are ways in which you can cope with or resolve such problems:

1. Don't try to avoid conflict by using the silent treatment. If you can't deal with the conflict immediately, set aside a time when you can talk later.

2. Don't save "emotional trading stamps." That is, don't let your feelings build until you end up with a deeper, more serious conflict.

3. If possible, prepare the setting for discussion. Most conflicts are much easier to work through if you can set the time, place and setting for discussion.

4. Attack the problem, not each other. Back up accusations with facts.

5. Don't throw your feelings like stones. Remember to forget. Describe your feelings, but refrain from using your feelings to gain an emotional or argumentative edge.

6. Stay on the subject. Discussion about conflicts generally moves away from the conflict itself and centers on accusations.

7. Offer solutions with your criticisms. Think through the criticism carefully.

8. Don't make extreme accusations. Avoid saying, "You never . . ." or "You always . . ."

9. Be humble. You could be wrong.

10. Don't attempt to manipulate others in the conflict by making statements such as "It's all my fault!"

Conflicts can be more easily dealt with if you can properly define the problem.

The following tips will help you to analyze the situation and move toward a solution:

1. Recognize the conflict issues. What really caused the problem?

2. Listen carefully to the other person describe the conflict. Ask clarifying questions. Summarize the conversation.

3. Carefully define the conflict:
- How do you think the other person(s) defines the problem?
- What behaviors of yours contribute to the conflict?
- What behaviors do you think the other person(s) sees as contributing to the problem?
- What are the issues of agreement and disagreement?

4. Identify alternative solutions to the conflict. List at least three different potential solutions.

5. Decide on one mutually acceptable solution.
- List the steps needed to implement the solution.
- Discuss the possible outcomes.
- List possible roadblocks to the solution.
- Discuss possible recourses that can make the solution possible.

6. Implement the new solution. Work on new behaviors. Keep the channels of communication open.

—*Gary Richardson*

____ Who's really leading the group, the officers or the adult leader?

____ Why do we always have to ask for permission from the church council to do anything?

____ Why can't we raise additional money the way we want to?

____ Why does the pastor have to "okay" everything before we do it?

____ Our group needs to be more "spiritual."

____ Our group needs to be more "social," to attract more people.

____ We always have to do it his way.

____ We don't communicate well enough with each other.

____ We never do anything new.

____ Nobody ever comes.

____ Why do we have to meet with the younger kids?

____ We never discuss anything exciting.

____ Where is God in all this?

● As soon as you've written your main concerns and frustrations, take a look at the list. Have everyone choose three items that cause most of the power struggles in the group. Mark them on the list and see what items get the most votes.

● Group the major concerns under these five headings: schedules, priorities, issues, needs and God. If certain concerns don't fit under any of those categories, make up a new one.

● Discuss ways to work together, youth and adults, on these concerns.

● Discuss the question, "What could each person do to make this concern go away?" Think about what can turn this negative into a positive.

● When these thoughts have been shared, make specific plans to remain aware of the tensions that can mount between adult leaders and young people. Close your meeting with a prayer for God's help to deal with tensions again when they surface.

ADDITIONAL READING

Caring Enough to Confront, David Augsburger, Regal Books.

Creative Conflict, Richard L. Krebs, Augsburg.

This practical self-inventory based on 1 Corinthians 13 will help you put love to work at repairing a damaged relationship.

How to Heal
A Relationship

BY LARRY KEEFAUVER

Everyone knows that relationships are essential in youth work. But anyone who has worked with kids for some time knows that relationships are often damaged. How can we heal relationships?

We can start by admitting that love is not a gushy feeling. Love is a decision to treat a person the way God says—regardless of our feelings.

Love also is not an abstract thought but a concrete action. If you are having problems with your love life, the following inventory from 1 Corinthians 13 is a way to focus specifically on repairing relationships. Decide which attribute of love you are having problems with and follow these instructions to heal that relationship.

Name a person you find difficult to love: _____

1. Love is patient.
   a. How long will it take, if you work at it, to develop a caring and acting love for this person?

b. Will you work on the relationship that long?

c. When will you start?

2. Love is kind.

a. List 10 positive statements you can say to that person to build his or her esteem:

b. When will you have said the 10 comments?

c. List 10 acts of kindness that you will do for that person:

d. When will you have completed them?

3. Love is not jealous.

a. What other persons compete for this person's love?

b. Do you resent any of them?

c. If so, when will you seek God's forgiveness and theirs for your resentment?

4. Love is not boastful.

a. Would it embarrass you to tell this person that you love him or her?

b. If yes, what in your pride needs to be broken so that you can say, "I love you"?

_____ fear   _____ hate

_____ bitterness   _____ other

When will you surrender this to God?

c. When will you say "I love you"?

5. Love is not arrogant or rude.

a. What things are you critical about in the person's behavior or personality?

b. God can enable us and others to change. We do not have the power to change others. Will you now surrender your criticism of the other person to God and write a prayer doing so?

c. List the times you have been rude to this person in the past week (put-downs, negative remarks, lack of attention, etc.).

d. What will you do this week to change your behavior?

6. Love does not insist on its own way.

a. What are three compromises you are willing to make so that the relationship will work?

Care Cards Build Warmth

Criticism and put-downs are too-common "fruits" among congregations. Their rotten flavor can poison a church. Here's a small tip that can help people build each other up. Send "Encouragement Cards" to each other. Here's a model for an encouragement card:

ENCOURAGEMENT CARD

"Therefore encourage one another, and build up one another, just as you also are doing."—1 Thessalonians 5:11

Guidelines: 1. Be brief
2. Be positive
3. Be sincere

Message to_____

from_____

(Please write message on reverse side and place in the offering plate.)

Of course, the above is only a model. Youth groups should find this a useful and meaningful tool for youth worship services. People enjoy giving and receiving the notes.

In the youth group setting, encouragement cards are especially effective. Tack big manila envelopes on a bulletin board, one for each member. Ask each member to write an encouragement card for every person in the group. Then put the cards in the appropriate envelopes. At the end of the meeting, give them their cards as they leave for home.

Youth leaders might send encouragement cards from time to time to the youth, group sponsors, senior pastor, church secretary— whoever needs encouragement.

Everyone loves encouragement. And, this card tip helps shyer people express themselves by the written word. The result may surprise you. There may be sudden warmth where there had been frosty criticism.

---

7. **Love is not irritable or resentful.**
   a. What irritates you most about the person?
   b. How can God use this irritation to refine your attitudes?
   c. Thank God for that irritation.

8. **Love does not rejoice at wrong, but rejoices in the right.**
   a. List 10 reasons you can praise God for letting you know this person.

9. Meditate on: **"Love hears all things, believes all things, hopes all things, endures all things. Love never ends."**

ADDITIONAL READING

Caring Enough to Forgive, David Augsburger, Herald.
Friend to Friend, J. David Stone and Larry Keefauver, Group Books.

You can nurture commitment and involvement of the young people in your group. Use these ideas to help kids take charge of their own ministry.

Helping Youth To Take Charge

BY JIM GREEN

Tom had been a youth director for eight months when he asked his group to help him paint three of the church's Sunday school rooms. Most of the youth group showed enthusiasm and readily agreed to help. Tom bought paint, brushes, dropcloths and cleaning materials. He cleaned up an old barbecue so that he could fix hamburgers for the kids for lunch. Can you imagine how Tom felt when only one member of the youth group showed up?

Sue asked two girls who she thought were dependable to get a mailing out to the youth group about a weekend social activity. It wasn't until a day before the event that she discovered the mail hadn't gone out, and the activity had to be canceled.

In both of these situations, the youth group members gave seemingly legitimate excuses for why they didn't fulfill their commitments. But Tom and Sue couldn't help but wonder what they were doing wrong.

We've all felt at times like Tom and Sue in our work with youth. But the questions remain: Why aren't kids more committed? How can you get them to take charge of their own ministry?

WHY AREN'T KIDS MORE COMMITTED?

Young people's commitment to the home has deteriorated to the point that hard work is almost non-existent. Responsibility is a word that only causes tension, and a responsibility to do a chore on time and do it right is often just an exercise in futility.

Teachers give assignments and tests, knowing that many assignments will be done at the last moment and tests seem to be mere exercises to be tolerated.

Employers are unsure of how much pressure to put on their teenage employees, and often end up catering to their whims and wants.

Coaches come the closest in receiving commitment from athletes who choose to participate in various sports, but over the past few years, many students have opted not to participate because the demands seemed too great.

Churches often make few demands on high school or junior high young people in their spiritual growth or responsibilities.

Thirty years ago few professional youth directors existed to run youth groups. Anything that happened in the youth group took place because either volunteers or the kids themselves made it happen. Today, with our director-centered youth ministries, kids have little or no need to be committed to the group.

Today's young people hesitate to accept responsibility. If you ask them for a commitment, they may ask themselves the questions: What are the rewards? What if something better comes up? How would doing this benefit me? Why should I commit myself?

HOW CAN YOU GET KIDS TO TAKE CHARGE?

I am a strong believer in young people and their talents and abilities. I have seen them travel to foreign countries to represent God in music and word. I have seen them work in the dirt and filth as they gave of themselves in the Dominican Republic, in Haiti and in the slums of our Appalachian

Mountains. I have seen them give strong leadership in churches and on campuses. I know they are capable of dedicated commitment.

Commitment *can* be taught. Here are a few ways you can teach it to your young people:

1. Be a role model.

Show the youth your level of commitment: fulfill your responsibilities without complaining, do more than you're asked, show initiative and motivation, keep your word, assist them and help them without asking for anything in return, and carry out your end of the bargain without being late or sloppy. As they begin to see commitment in action, they will visualize what could be required of them.

In 1 Thessalonians 1:6 Paul says, "You become imitators of us and of the Lord." In John 13:14 Jesus said, "As I washed your feet, you are to wash one another's feet, and I have given you this as an example."

2. Encourage your young people.

A teacher friend of mine agreed to teach a group of hyperactive and unresponsive third graders.

My friend's opening comment to them was: "I'm glad you're here, and I want you in my class for three reasons. First, you're the brightest and smartest kids I've seen. Second, you are sensitive and caring for each other like I've never seen before. Third, your ability to study independently of others will be a delight to experience."

He told them this every day, and they soon began to believe it. At the end of the year, his class of "expendables" rated an entire grade point average higher in their testing than the other third grade classes. They turned out to be one of the best groups of students to ever go through the third grade at that school.

Tell your young people you believe in them. Give encouragement. Remind them that with their abilities and talents they will have an influence in their homes, on campus and in the world.

Keep telling them they're good.

3. Build their confidence and self-esteem.

Let your young people do things. First give them small jobs

with short-term success goals. Then open greater responsibilities to them. Don't be afraid to be specific when asking for commitment. For instance, Tom (who wanted help painting Sunday school rooms) could have asked one student to be responsible for mixing and preparing the paint, assigned another to take care of the brushes and rollers, and asked another to prepare lunch.

Present responsibilities in a straightforward manner. List any difficulties and rewards of particular tasks that need to be done. Don't make a task seem easier than it really is in order to get a volunteer; that may lead to feelings of resentment and guilt on the part of the young person when a task is not carried out.

Commitment must be set up in a way that each young person knows that if he or she doesn't do it, the task will not get done. In essence, we're talking about consequences of actions: praise for a job well done, recognition and a good feeling—or that horrible nagging feeling that results from letting people down.

Take the time to review each level of responsibility so group members know that you know what needs to be done. Remember: Practice doesn't make perfect, practice makes permanent. As you give young people responsibility and leadership, that practice will become permanent in their lifestyles and in their commitments.

4. Talk with your young people about commitment.

Discuss what it means to take charge. What do the kids think they should be committed to: activities and events? the church? you? themselves? God? Why do your group members think you ask for their commitment: you want their loyalty? to make your job easier? you want to help them become all they can be? you want their respect? Why do kids sometimes agree to responsibilities they don't want: peer pressure? fear of losing your friendship? Try to find their real reasoning.

Avoid creating too much hype and promotion around an event or task, trying to convince kids it's fun and exciting and that they absolutely should be involved. Let them know it's okay and understandable to hesitate before giving themselves to service, since it's wise to count the costs before plunging headlong into any commitment.

Your young people are capable of commitment. With time and patience, you can teach them about commitment—its difficulties and rewards. When group members visualize long-range results for their efforts and take ownership for events and projects, they'll begin to know commitment.

Be a model for your kids, encourage them, build their confidence and self-esteem, and talk to them openly and honestly about commitment. They'll thank you for it.

ADDITIONAL READING

Servant-Leaders in the Making, Les Christie, Victor.

Volunteer Youth Workers: Recruiting and Developing Leaders for Youth Ministry, J. David Stone and Rose Mary Miller, Group Books.

Things do go wrong in your programs for young people. Patience and humor go a long way in setting a Christian example.

Whatever Can Go Wrong . . .

BY BEN SHARPTON

It was 8:30 on the Saturday evening of our church's Youth Weekend, and everyone had gathered in the sanctuary for a worship. As our special guest speaker delivered his message, I slipped outside to set up for an outdoor movie which was to follow the service. Sometime between the speaker's second and third points, the projection table tipped, and projector, table, three reels of film and a takeup reel crashed to the ground.

Miraculously, the film remained intact, but the projector (and my spirits) was broken beyond immediate repair.

The projector ordeal wasn't the first (or last) of that weekend's catastrophes. My wife, who had been called out of town because of a death in the family, received a speeding ticket; one of the volunteer leaders failed to show up; the special music hadn't been rehearsed and sounded terrible—and so did the worship service. That's not all: The church air conditioning was on the blink; my car's alternator went out; the final reel of the movie arrived backward; and the young people decorated the church lawn with popcorn which had to be swept up before the Sunday worship services.

Later that night as I wound the movie by hand, I realized that things had felt out of control. My efforts to provide a flawless activity had failed. Despite the fact that I had covered all the bases, planned far enough in advance, delegated responsibilities, and followed up properly, things had gone wrong.

That's the way youth work is. If you plan a cookout, it will probably rain. If you organize a swimming party, the weather will turn cold. Your high school football team will go to the state tournament—for the first time in 30 years—on the same weekend as your church ski trip. If you order a film, you can reckon that it will be shown on television the night before your showing.

EXPECT IT

Things go wrong. It's a fact of life and one of the consequences of the Fall of Man. If man were not separated from his creator, Murphy's Law (Whatever Can Go Wrong, Will Go Wrong) wouldn't exist. When a wedding has been scheduled during the youth concert, or the curriculum order is late, or the church bus breaks down again, you can always blame someone.

And, in youth work, there are many folks to use as scapegoats. Satan probably gets more credit than he deserves. Parents seem to lose their senses when their children reach adolescence. Repeatedly, kids fail to do what they say they'll do. Church boards are rarely efficient and seldom effective (God so loved the world that he didn't send a committee).

But all too often, youth leaders themselves are not planning one more rehearsal or writing one more letter or scheduling one more hour of study or making one more visit. There's no excuse for surprises that come from poor planning. Your goal as youth leader is to plan and execute your ministry as best you can. The surprises should come as those unavoidable quirks of working with people and machines, not because you weren't prepared.

LAUGH IT OFF

Your attitude toward the unexpected can affect other aspects of your program. If you let a traffic jam get under your skin on the way to your group's "Hawaiian Luau," chances are your kids will roast more than the pig. On the other hand, if you take those surprises in stride, other people will reflect your flexible attitude. Kids can be forgiving; your attitude facilitates or inhibits their forgiveness. Patience and a little humor help maintain a healthy mood in your group.

THE BROAD VIEW

When things go wrong, it often helps to look at the situation objectively. What long-reaching effects will really occur because it rained during the cookout? Who will suffer most because the church P.A. system is on the blink? Is the execution of your program worth jeopardizing your relationship with one of your young people? What is really important— matters of the kingdom, or your own fragile ego? Perhaps it will be of greater value for your young people to see God pull you through those tough, unpredictable situations than to observe your polished, problem-free program.

Paul's missionary travels were enough to drive a person crazy. Paul was whipped, arrested, thrown in prison, stoned, betrayed, shipwrecked and almost assassinated. Things really went wrong! Yet, he still proclaimed: "I am content with weaknesses, hardships, persecutions and difficulties for Christ's sake. For when I am weak, then I am strong" (2 Corinthians 12:10).

Things will go wrong in your programs for young people. When they do, stop and take a deep breath, smile a little, set a good example and think of the broad view. And remember that when you are weak in your own power, you are strong in the power of Christ.

ADDITIONAL READING

Managing Yourself, Stephen B. Douglass, Here's Life.
Psycho-cybernetics, Maxwell Maltz, Prentice-Hall.

Use this test to analyze the
strengths and weaknesses
in your youth program and
in your leadership.

CHAPTER
14

Test Yourself On Your Goals For Youth Work

BY PAUL THOMPSON

At least twice a year you should try to take a fresh look at your youth ministry. Here's a brief evaluation form to help you think through where you have been and what direction you would like your youth ministry to take.

Remember that your score isn't as important as the new discoveries and creative ideas that emerge from this process.

Complete or check the appropriate spaces.

1. Name a current movie popular with your youth group: _____

   _____ ;

   a current song: _____.

2. Have you called any members in the past six months to find out why they've stopped attending?
   Yes☐   No☐

3. Check the topics listed below that you have dealt with as a group in the past six months:

sexuality	☐	world peace	☐
world hunger	☐	parental relations	☐
vocational guidance	☐	dating or intimacy	☐
communication	☐	drug and alcohol abuse	☐
prejudice	☐	friendship	☐
teenage suicide	☐	spiritual growth	☐

4. Do you keep a bulletin board of newspaper clippings recognizing your group members' achievements?
   Yes☐   No☐

5. Have any of your young people brought a friend to a recent activity?
   Yes☐   No☐
   Does this happen regularly?
   Yes☐   No☐

6. List three positive comments you've heard group members make since school started:
   A. _____
   B. _____
   C. _____

7. Have you (check the box if "yes"):
   eaten lunch at school with a group member?   ☐
   met with a group member for a soda after school?   ☐
   attended a school event where several young people
   from church were participating?   ☐

8. Do you use scripture in conjunction with at least half your activities?
   Yes☐   No☐

9. Check the topics listed below that you've dealt with as a group in the past six months:

forgiveness	☐	Christ's birth, life,	
grace	☐	death or Resurrection	☐
Christian ethics	☐	cost of discipleship	☐
guilt	☐	God's gifts	☐
being valued by God	☐		

10. Since school started, how many activities has your group completed in each of the following categories?
Worship ____ Education ____ Service ____ Fellowship ____

11. Has at least one of your activities involved the group with young people outside of your congregation?
Yes☐   No☐

12. Do you have at least one adult sponsor or leader who is new this year?
Yes☐   No☐

13. Have you read a new book, taken a class, or attended a training workshop in the past six months?
Yes☐   No☐

14. Has your group taken a trip or been part of a retreat in the past six months?
Yes☐   No☐

15. List one or more criticisms that you remember from this past fall:
A. _____
B. _____
C. _____
D. _____

Did you deal with them effectively and creatively?
Yes☐   No☐

16. Can you recall any group members saying something similar to, "I never thought of it in that way before"?
Yes☐   No☐

17. Have you tried an event, activity or program in the past six months that you didn't know whether it would succeed or fail?
Yes☐   No☐

18. Does your youth group have a published schedule of activities at least one month in advance?
Yes☐   No☐

19. Estimate the average amount of time you invest in the planning of each activity:
    30 minutes ☐ 90 minutes☐
    1 hour ☐ 2 hours or more☐

20. Is a young person from the youth group serving as a regular member of a church committee?
    Yes☐ No☐

21. Before you began this evaluation did you think of asking several young people to complete it as well?
    Yes☐ No☐

22. Has the youth group had a successful activity in the past six months without your being present?
    Yes☐ No☐

23. Have parents:
    helped with the details in the past few months? ☐
    been participants in a program in the past few months? ☐
    helped plan one or more activity? ☐

24. Do you feel that the percentage of your personal responsibility for the youth program is:
    greater than 50 percent? ☐
    equal to or less than 50 percent? ☐

SCORING

Give yourself one point for each completed blank or box you checked "yes" for questions 1, 2, 4, 5, 6, 8, 10, 11, 12, 13, 14, 15, 16, 17, 18, 20, 21 and 22. For questions 3, 7, 9 and 23, give yourself one point for each check, up to three checks a question. For question 19, give yourself one point if you checked any answer but 30 minutes. On question 24, give yourself a point if you checked equal to or less than 50 percent.

Questions 1 through 3 are related to staying in touch. Youth ministry is best when it relates to the lives and concerns of young people. Questions 4 through 7 center on affirmation. Giving and receiving affirmation is the business of the church. God sent Christ to let us know how much we matter. Do we let others know their importance with our words and presence? Bringing a friend (Question 5) is the greatest compliment a young person can give a youth leader. Questions 8 through 10 are questions of identity. We are not the YMCA, Scouts or a school activity. We are the church. A good balance of activities meets more needs (Question 10). Questions 11 through 13 concern staying fresh. A good youth program needs new ideas. Growth is the issue in questions 14 through 17. Are you and your group members becoming better people and having a better program through your experiences together? Good administration is a necessity; questions 18 and 19 are two important checkpoints of appropriate administration. Questions 20 through 24 center on ownership. Whom does the program involve and whose program is it?

Use the chart to score yourself. Remember that its main purpose is to help you to know more about strengths and weaknesses in your youth program and your leadership.

33-40	God's little acre.
23-32	Moving toward the kingdom.
13-22	Average Church USA.
Below 13	Time to come out of the wilderness.

ADDITIONAL READING

Management, Peter F. Drucker, Harper and Row.

Where's It At? The Measure of Your Youth Ministry, Gary Richardson, Victor.

Section 2

MANAGING YOUR RELATIONSHIPS WITH ADULTS INVOLVED IN YOUTH MINISTRY

Lighten your leadership
duties by sharing the
responsibilities of youth
ministry.

Sharing The Load: Team Ministry

BY GINNY WARD HOLDERNESS

One of the toughest challenges in ministry is planning and leading a weekly youth group meeting—especially when you have to do it by yourself.

When you follow a Lone Ranger style of leadership, it's easy to get burned out. You get little support and guidance when you have few resources and when you're left to sink or swim. Frustration builds each week as you have to "get up a program" without assistance.

You can eliminate this frustration and construct a program or ministry with youth that has purpose and continuity. "How?" you eagerly ask. By involving youth in the planning. In this participatory planning process, you and a team of leaders guide your youth in the selection of three or four activities in each of five areas of the life of the church:

● Worship—as a group or with the entire congregation.

● Study—exploration of topics, issues and Bible topics.

● Ministry within the congregation—all that young people do with and for older and younger members of the congregation.

● Servicing to those outside the congregation.

● Fellowship—recreation, socials, retreats, trips, group building.

At a fall planning retreat, the youth and leaders decide on these activities and schedule them on a calendar. The calendar gives everyone involved (church, parents, friends) an idea of "what the youth group will be like at our church."

Now the youth group is beyond mere study or recreation. Youth can be involved in the total life of the church. The youth group may have three studies a year, lasting three Sunday nights each. Service projects can be spread over the months and may include Saturdays or after-school hours. The youth have variety. They never end up doing the same activities meeting after meeting.

This design works well in many churches. It offers a structured planning process and suggests that kids be involved in planning in a more responsible way. (Much better than the old approach of, "Well, what do you want to do this year?")

But there's one problem. This multi-activity plan is too much for one leader. If activities are carried out in all the five areas (which include retreats, dramas, service projects, trips, creative worship experiences, special studies, projects with children and adult church members, and many more), you will have one exhausted leader!

JOIN THE TEAM

The need arises to involve more adults in youth ministry. Thus: *team ministry*. To recruit the necessary leaders, you need to have a clear structure of team ministry. To get leaders together to plan, it is wise to have an understanding of what you want to do in youth ministry.

The structure that I recommend involves youth in the total life of the church. To get this involvement of the young people, you need to recruit at least two leaders for each of these five areas of the church's life (two for worship, two for study, two for ministry within the congregation, two for service, and two to four for fellowship). You now share the ministry with a team of 10 to 12 adults. The leaders are only responsible for their specific areas. They don't need to attend every youth group event.

The team of adult leaders and the young people plan the

year's calendar at a planning retreat. The youth choose just three or four activities in each area, so each adult leader will actually be with the youth only six to nine times during the year. Result: no more overworked leaders. In fact, now the leaders are free to spend leisure time with the youth on nights when they are not responsible for the leadership. They are free to enjoy building relationships with the kids.

BENEFITS OF TEAM MINISTRY

Think of the benefits of a team-oriented youth ministry:

1. You don't have to go it alone.

2. There is a built-in support group working together on the same task.

3. You can specialize. Persons who love camping but are afraid of leading a Bible study can work in the fellowship area. Another person who has an interest in worship, but none in canoeing, skiing and such, can be on the worship team. People can use their talents in one area and not feel pressured to "do it all."

4. The youth get to know more adults in the church. Often the only adult members they know are their leaders, church school teachers and friends of their parents.

5. More adults say yes when recruited, because of:
● the lesser time commitment
● the support of the church and other leaders
● the knowledge that they are recruited to a specific area
● the enthusiasm of a team effort
● less fear of failure

6. When you have that many adults excited about the youth, the kids know somebody cares. And that fact alone can revolutionize your youth ministry.

THE TEAM COORDINATOR

An important element in the team is the coordinator. Any group of leaders needs someone to serve as the "ultimate responsible person." One person needs to call the team together, set up the planning retreat or meeting, and make those dozens of phone calls to ascertain that the leaders remember what their responsibilities are and when they're supposed to do them.

I recommend one coordinator for the senior highs and one for the junior highs. These two work closely together. They keep each other aware of various emphases in the life of the church (such as mission, stewardship, Advent, Lent), so that the youth may be given opportunities to take part. The coordinators should be in close touch with the church staff. In fact, a minister, a full-time youth leader, or a director of Christian education could coordinate one of the leadership teams.

The leaders need to be aware that what they are doing is of vital importance in the life of the church. People will know what is happening with youth at their church when they see a number of enthusiastic adults involved.

GET STARTED

Move carefully as you incorporate team ministry in your church. Team ministry is a large undertaking that needs time to develop. It needs a lot of preparation and publicity before a team is even recruited. If this process of ministry is to work well, the staff, minister, church school teachers, present youth group leaders and youth need to be included in the early discussion.

Many churches have trouble with team ministry because the team receives little guidance as to how to set up a youth ministry. And, little effort is made to interpret youth ministry to the congregation.

If you would like to revamp your youth program by moving toward a team ministry, appoint a task force of five to nine individuals to be in charge of getting this concept started. Assign several youth to the task force, as well as a couple of parents and a member of the church board. This group will be responsible for the following preliminaries:

1. Clarify the purpose and structure of youth ministry. This group should examine the present involvement of youth in the life of the church and discuss what it would like to see happen with the youth in the church.

2. Recruit the coordinators.

3. Set up a calendar. Determine a date by which leaders should be recruited. Set dates for the orientation and training of leaders, the planning retreat, and for a special meeting of parents and youth.

4. Recruit leaders. Decide who will do the recruiting. A few tips: Make sure recruiting is done through personal conversations, not by telephone. Keep away from the high

pressure salesmanship. Let prospective leaders in on what the hopes are for youth ministry at your church. Share your enthusiasm. Let them express in which areas they have interests or talents. Ask them for suggestions of other people who might be possible leaders.

5. Communicate this approach to the congregation. This is the factor which makes possible a successful youth ministry. If you want more for your youth than a string of Sunday night "programs," if you really want a church that has an *active* group of youth, then work needs to be done in communicating and interpreting youth ministry to the congregation. If the members are aware of the total youth ministry, then they can support you. In fact, they can get excited and brag on what "we're doing with our youth." Every church *says* the youth are a high priority.

6. Begin training the leaders. Team coordinators should set up sessions to help the leaders be more effective in their areas. An individual with skills in Christian education and youth ministry can lead training sessions on: ascertaining age group characteristics, relating to youth, finding and using resources, and developing faith.

Getting started takes time. But even with three advisers you can use the five-area plan—double up on the responsibilities. Remember that this is a limited version. You cannot expect the level of team enthusiasm or youth response as you would have with a whole team. However, you can start with a limited version and work toward implementing the full team approach in the coming year.

THE FIRST YEAR CAN BE ROUGH

Even if you've spent months preparing for the new thrust in youth ministry, let me assure you that the first year can be rough. You may not get the youth response you expected. There may be many snags with the team. (Failure to communicate is one.) The second year will be better! Don't give up because your plans didn't work as well as you had expected. By the second year, the congregation will have an idea of what is going on and the youth will be used to the change in structure.

Because leaders are no longer overworked, they will be more willing to work with the team the second and third year. You may need to replace one or two, but you won't have to start all over.

After four years of team ministry at Shelby Presbyterian Church, Shelby, North Carolina, we had 43 adults (in a church of 600) who had been trained and had experience on the youth ministry team. It is a joy to see youth interacting with a variety of personalities and styles of adult leadership. It is rewarding to be a part of a congregation in which youth actively participate in all aspects of the church's life.

ADDITIONAL READING

Starting a Youth Ministry, Larry Keefauver, Group Books.

Volunteer Youth Workers: Recruiting and Developing Leaders for Youth Ministry, J. David Stone and Rose Mary Miller, Group Books.

Youth Ministry: The New Team Approach, Ginny Ward Holderness, John Knox.

Parents can help you increase your ministry's effectiveness. Here are seven ways to tap this resource.

Do You Need More Support From Kids' Parents?

BY PAUL BORTHWICK

For many of us, the idea of parental support in youth ministry is frightening. The demanding parents who expect that we will mend the rifts between them and their teenagers come to mind. The parents who welcome us to the youth group with, "Let's see how long you will last!" send chills down our spines. The grateful parents who state, "I'm so glad you are the leader; I am confident that you can help my Johnny," remind us that some parents hope we will be miracle workers.

Excessive demands. Unrealistic expectations. Unjustified criticisms. All these things keep us from wanting to work with parents, but we must.

If our desire is for more than a "fun 'n games" youth ministry, if we hope for long-term effects in the lives of youth, if we truly desire to minister to youth, we must get the parents to help us. It is their values, attitudes and relationships that will have the greatest long-term effects on youth. To build our youth ministries without concern for the parents is to neglect the most influential people in the lives of our youth. When we realize that our efforts in youth ministry complement (or, in some cases, contradict) the foundations built in the home, we can begin to understand our need to get parental support.

Without parental support, we may be mistrusted or put into competition with the home. The combination, however, of our natural fear of parents and of the parents' panic as they see their "darlings" enter adolescence often makes this support difficult to find.

Based on my experience and the experience of others whom I have observed, I have come to the conclusion that parents tend to offer their support based on how we present ourselves. Here are seven suggestions to help:

COMMIT YOURSELF TO THE YOUTH

The parents want us to be advocates of the youth; they want to know that we have their children's best interests in mind. For this reason, a long-term commitment to youth ministry is certainly one of the bases on which trust can be built with the parents because they see that we are deeply committed to helping teenagers grow and mature into full, responsible adulthood. (Note: This factor, therefore, gives an additional challenge to the youth leader who has assumed leadership of a group that has had three youth leaders in the past two years. Inasmuch as that leader will be challenged to build the trust of the teenagers, he or she will face an equal challenge with the parents.)

COMMUNICATE WITH THE PARENTS

If we are secretive about the youth ministry or the program, parents will get suspicious. We must let them know what's happening in the youth group. We also must communicate to parents that we are willing to listen to them; ignoring their wisdom and experience will cause us to sacrifice a great deal of insights into working with youth.

BE RESOURCEFUL REGARDING YOUTH

In many cases, parents are "out of touch" with the teenage world. When we offer some of our observations, parents usually are open to listening. The effective youth leader realizes, "Hey, I do know something about today's teenager, and parents could benefit from what I know."

In our youth ministry, this "resourcefulness" has taken the form of parents' seminars (90 minutes) every other month. We have addressed teenage music, peer pressure, sexual activity, handling money and financing a college education. Each seminar includes a time for questions as well as a time for presenting other related books and resources.

Other youth ministries distribute newsletters to parents to publicize trends among teenagers, suggestions for improving relationships at home and the upcoming youth ministry schedule. One great resource possibility in almost any church is other parents. Opening doors of communication among parents of teenagers helps them to share their wisdom, recognize that they are not alone in their problems and give support to each other.

BE SENSITIVE TO PARENTS' NEEDS

Parents' critical words or high expectations often are caused by one basic problem: Parents see themselves as failing, and—unable to handle the guilt alone—they blame the youth leader, pastor, school teachers or anyone else who happens to be around.

For those of us without teenage children, it is difficult to imagine the pressures and fears parents experience as their children grow up. Some handle it well; others crack under the load. John White, in his book **Parents in Pain** (InterVarsity Press, Downers Grove, Illinois), describes the home where crisis is occurring:

Storms of unbelievable ferocity can turn homes into disaster areas. In some households the emotional climate is rarely free from weather warnings. Instead of the gentleness and kindness that ought to prevail, bitterness, rage, resentment, and sorrow sweep through the household. In the wake of each storm, though calm may seem to dominate, stormy passions continue to rage inside the hearts of individual family members.

The youth leader who aspires to win the support of parents must be willing and prepared to be a sounding board, a counselor or a support to parents who are in great pain.

Sensitivity to parents' needs may also mean being cautious with our youth activity schedule: Parents are appreciative when we don't over-schedule (and take the youth away from home too often), when we set times that reflect a thoughtfulness for family meals, and when we schedule activities well in advance (especially in the summer so that family vacations can be planned).

SUPPORT THE FAMILY UNIT

The youth leader who always sides with the youth against the parents will fail. Promoting an "us vs. them" mentality is destructive.

Supporting the family unit means that we don't believe every word from our teenagers. One girl came to me and complained that her mother "beat" her. In a world of great child abuse, I was concerned. I realized, however, that this 16-year-old was quite capable of exaggerating. With a few more questions, I learned that the mother had slapped the girl—once—in response to a sassy, swear-filled outburst. I was glad that I hadn't overreacted to the girl's initial story.

Supporting the family unit might also mean that we encourage young people to be obedient. When the whole youth group wants to go to a movie, but one parent says "no" to his or her teenager, our response is important. We must—if we are to promote familial harmony—support the decisions of the parents even if we don't always agree.

We also can support the family unit by letting the youth group members know our spouses and children. Our influence as husband or wife and parent will be more effective when the youth see us interact in a family setting.

RESPOND FIRMLY TO PARENTS

Parents need us to be realistic. A friend of mine took on a youth ministry in which there were many disillusioned "church kids." In this first month, he met with the parents. "I am here to do my best under God," he told them, "but I am not a miracle worker. If you want someone who can work miracles with your teenagers in a few short months, you have hired the wrong man."

Although some parents were shocked at his candor, they understood exactly what he was saying (he has stayed at that church for four years, and by God's grace, he has "worked some miracles"). Parents need us to be realistic about the harsh problems that many of them are facing. They don't need a glib "God will work it all out" from us

WHAT ABOUT PARENTAL INVOLVEMENT?

Perhaps some of us are not so fearful of getting parental support as we are of getting parents involved. I don't mind telling parents about our "All-Nighter," but to have them *involved* in the event (where they might pass judgment on my leadership and on the wisdom of my decisions) can be intimidating.

But remember that while support from parents is essential, their involvement is optional. In considering it, ask, "How involved?" Will we invite parents to an activity once a year or every week?

If we want to have parents involved as regular participants, we must consider these pros and cons: On the pro side, parental involvement can fill our need for adult leaders and offer insights into youth that can't be found in books. If many youth group members are from single-parent families, having parents regularly involved might meet a great need in their lives.

The opposing viewpoint, however, is that parental involvement can bring an element of discomfort for those parents, for their children in the group and for the youth leader. The parents might feel overprotective; the youth, cramped; and the youth leader, caught within the tension. Take the needs of the young people into account before deciding to involve parents.

when they are experiencing a disaster. They are saying, "Look, we are in deep trouble; can you help at all?"

In our firmness, we need to help parents to not overreact. Some feel that they are "the only ones who have ever experienced this problem," and we need to help them see that there are others in the same predicament. We are also the ones who can reassure parents that they have not "wasted their lives" because a 15-year-old son has started smoking.

Firm responses to parents might also include a challenge to them about their own spiritual growth. I regularly tell the parents of our youth that their attitudes about God and church will be picked up by their teenagers. One of my

If we choose to have parents involved in the youth ministry, what will they do? Here are five roles parents can fill:

Participants. Invite parents to come into the youth ministry in a friendly, non-authoritative role. Father/son or mother/daughter athletics, meals or even cooperative service projects can build the relationships between teenagers and parents in a relatively non-threatening environment.

Leaders. It is possible to have parents as youth leaders, if both youth and parents agree; however, parents need to allow their teenage children to be normal participants in the group.

"Occasional experts." Use parents as speakers and panel participants when discussing careers, college options or even the problems of parenting.

Advisers to the youth leader. We have had parents serve (representing the broadest spectrum of the families of our church) on a parents advisory board which tells me how the youth group members are responding, which needs we are failing to meet, and ways that we can improve.

Resources to each other. One of the most effective type of ministry that I have seen among the parents of our youth has been done by *other* parents of youth. Teaching, counseling or consoling occurs most effectively when parents go to each other for help.

favorite summaries goes like this: "In our youth group, I will be challenging our teenagers to have a daily time to read the Bible, pray and grow with God. I will encourage them to witness at school and at work and to pray for their friends. But I should tell you (parents) that these things rarely happen in the life of the young person over the long haul if they are not being exemplified at home. For this reason, I urge you to be growing, witnessing and living for Christ in your own life as the primary example to your teenagers."

BUILD BRIDGES BETWEEN YOUTH AND PARENTS

In the book of Ezekiel, God looks for someone who will

"stand in the gap" between himself and the people, someone to be a bridge-builder between those who are at odds
with each other.

Parents and young people need youth workers who will
stand in the gap. The supportiveness of parents occurs when
they see us in that role, seeking to serve both them and their
children.

Being bridge-builders means that we teach parents how to
understand their teenagers and the world in which they live.
Being bridge-builders also means that we openly challenge
young people to love and care for their parents.

Whether this "bridge-building" function means encouraging parents to go on the high school campus or helping youth
write notes of appreciation to their parents, it will require
work and creativity on our part. Yet it is worth it, for the
parents and teenagers will "graduate" from the youth
group, but they will always have each other.

Effectiveness in youth ministry means that we—the youth
leaders—reach out to both students and parents. Drawing
families together, teaching youth to be responsible as young
adults and yet respectful as children, and helping parents to
"let go" of their teenagers as they mature will not be easy.
Nevertheless, we must practice these ways of gaining support from parents so that our youth ministries will be reaching those who have the maximum effect on teenagers—the
parents.

ADDITIONAL READING

Five Cries of Parents, Merton P. Strommen, Harper and
Row.

Parents and Teenagers, various authors, Victor.

Conflicts with parents can be eased or avoided if you remember two components: prevention and management.

CHAPTER
17

Friend or Foe: How Do You Relate to Parents?

BY LARRY KEEFAUVER

Have you ever heard parents say: "They are never serious."

"Our youth don't get enough Bible at our church. What's wrong with our youth ministry (or more often, our youth minister)?"

"The youth never leave or return from an outing on time. The parents have to wait in the church parking lot for hours."

"Our youth minister seems to relate only to certain popular kids in our youth group. He never spends time with my son."

"You have no business confronting or correcting my child at the youth meetings."

"The youth program in our church doesn't begin to compare with the one down at First Church. We're going to take our teenagers there if things here don't improve!"

Or, there's the pressure when the pastor comes to you and says: "I've been getting a number of complaints about your handling of So-and-so in the youth group. The parents have asked me to talk with you and get the problem solved."

How do you handle conflicts with parents? Which of the following responses sound the most like you:

I avoid the problem. After all, with time all things heal or are forgotten.

I set the parents straight. I give them the facts and persuade them to realize they are wrong.

I get the youth on my side. I convince the youth to win over their parents to my view. Or, I get the youth to side with me against their parents.

I refer the problem to a committee or higher authority. I have the education committee, the youth coordinator or youth council, or the pastor handle the conflict.

Each of us may have tried one or all of the preceding responses at one time or another. While they may have helped us dodge a few punches, these approaches are ineffective and usually destructive. Let's consider two dimensions of handling conflict with parents: prevention and management.

PREVENT CONFLICT

Building positive relationships with parents effectively prevents or lessens conflict. This preventative maintenance program requires constant awareness and commitment to make it work.

Communicate. Many parents become agitated when they don't know or understand what's happening in the youth program. Don't rely only on the youth themselves to handle your communication with the parents. Direct communication is the best.

Communicate through:
- church bulletins and newsletters
- regular youth newsletters or post cards
- direct mailings and phone calls to the parents
- home visitations.

Before one ski trip, all the youth sponsors in our church took information to the homes of the youth and parents. We explained the details and answered questions. It was the smoothest trip we ever planned. We avoided many potential problems through face-to-face communication.

Listen. Pay attention when parents express their needs and concerns. Don't refer them to someone else; take them seriously. When rumors of conflict reach you, listen closely and then go directly to the source. In fact, ask for constructive criticism and suggestions about how to have a more effective youth ministry program.

Conduct parent meetings. Two or three times a year, we have a covered-dish meeting with all the parents. We discuss upcoming youth activities on the youth calendar, provide information about the resources and curriculum we are using, and invite parents to share any questions or concerns.

Solicit parent involvement. We had one parent couple who continually criticized our Sunday evening youth meetings. I insisted that they assist the sponsors for a few Sunday evenings. That met with such a positive response that over the years we have invited parents to youth programs and events to observe what happens.

Conflict often arises when parents feel neglected, left out, sidestepped and put down. Youth ministry is more than just working with youth. It is ministry with youth and their parents.

MANAGE CONFLICT

In spite of our best efforts at prevention, conflict does arise. I mentioned earlier some destructive steps in handling conflict with parents. Now for positive coping with conflict:

Listen. We communicate empathy, understanding, worth and concern when we listen seriously and attentively to one another. The scripture gives us insight, "Let everyone be quick to listen, slow to speak, slow to anger" (James 1:19). A parent may need to ventilate hostility before constructive dialogue can occur. Don't interrupt the person talking. Ask only questions that seek to clarify, not intimidate.

Avoid defensiveness. A.W. Tozer in his "Five Spiritual Vows" says that Christians should never defend themselves since God is our rock and our strong defense (Psalm 59:9, 17). It's one thing to speak the truth quietly without putting the other person down, it's another to become defensive to the point that we attack or allow ourselves to become hostile.

Determine who owns the problem. This simple skill from the Parent Effectiveness Training program is applicable to conflict with parents. A parent was having tremendous discipline problems at home with her teenager. Yet, whenever her son caused problems at youth meetings, she felt he was

innocent and blamed me for the problem. After months of
simmering conflict with his parent, I asked both mother and
son to join me for a three-way discussion. We resolved who
was responsible for what and agreed to future consequences at home and church for the teenager when destructive behavior happened again.

Accept responsibility for your mistakes. Yes, youth ministers and workers do make mistakes. Should we forget,
Romans 3:23 provides a good reminder. All sides bear some
responsibility for most conflicts. Face your weaknesses honestly and openly. Parents will develop deep respect for you
when you admit your own vulnerability.

Face conflict directly and personally. When I know that
parents have a problem with me, I go directly to them. I
want to hear from the source about the conflict as soon as
possible. No one else can face my problem for me.

Some conflicts need to be discussed in committees or with
the pastor to fully resolve the problem and avoid its recur-
rence. Still, the first step is to face the conflict yourself.

When the problem is yours, ask for forgiveness. Again
the Bible gives us insight. "Confess your sins to one
another" (James 5:16). Simply saying "I'm sorry" is often in-
sipid. Ask the parent, "Will you forgive me for . . .?" Jesus
in the Sermon on the Mount teaches that we are to seek reconciliation with our brother before going to the altar. How
often I have sat in church stewing over a conflict with a
parent when I needed to ask forgiveness.

GOOD NEWS

I have good news for you. Every conflict with parents can
be a learning, growing experience. We can face problems
with parents as possibilities for deepening our relationships
with them and experiencing God's grace.

ADDITIONAL READING

Bringing Up Children in the Christian Faith, John H. West-
erhoff III, Winston-Seabury.

Christians in Families, Roy Fairchild, John Knox.

Youth ministry involves
more than its share of
problems. Here are a few
ideas to help you cope.

CHAPTER
18

Dealing With Frustrations In Leadership

BY LEE SPARKS

Check the following if they apply to you:

☐Have you poured yourself into youth ministry for a time yet felt you haven't even *started* to reach your kids?

☐Does attendance at meetings vary radically?

☐Are your fingernails chewed down to the quick?

☐Are there occasional miffs (or even cold wars) between the pastor, parents or church leaders, or combinations thereof, and the youth program?

☐Do your members readily commit themselves to projects, only to neglect or forget what they agreed to do?

One youth leader answered "yes" to most of these questions. He often came home from youth activities angered and hurt by the constant barrage of frustrations. "I felt like dying," he said.

For some youth leaders, *frustration* is a synonym for youth ministry. Like the harried leader, frustrations can get us down.

You don't have to spend much time reading the Bible to find people who seemed to prefer death to overwhelming frustration. Though he was not a youth leader, Moses knew firsthand the frustrations of leading God's people. The first 10 chapters of the book of Numbers illustrate the glory and spectacle as Israel prepares for its march toward the Promised Land. The tribes are assembled and accounted for. Finally, the trumpets blow, and the people set off.

Then, in abrupt contrast, the next chapter tells of the people's constant complaints. Moses, in a fit of frustration, realizes that he cannot find food for the people. Seeing no way to fulfill the expectations placed on him, Moses turns in his resignation. "I can't be responsible for all these people by myself; it's too much for me! If you are going to treat me like this, have pity on me and kill me, so that I won't have to endure your cruelty any longer," Moses bellows at God (Numbers 11:14-15). Moses would rather be dead than face seemingly impossible leadership pressures.

MOSES AND YOU

Youth ministry is a "Moses" type of leadership. It is a frustrating business. Let's glance at some built-in pressures nearly every youth leader encounters.

● In most churches, youth ministry is seen as a second-class need. Full-time associate ministers are often assigned "second-class" tasks, usually youth work and Christian education. These associates tend to receive second-class support for their ministries. Or, youth ministers are seen as preparing for "real" ministry later. Adult volunteers often grudgingly agree to help. Lay and part-time workers find their evenings and weekends filled to overflowing with the personal and programming needs of their youth.

● Youth leaders usually only have one or two hours a week to make a difference in a young person's 168-hour week. Want to see how little time you might actually spend with your youth? Measure out 168 inches of string and mark one or two inches (even three or four) in the middle. That's how little time you have to spend with your kids compared with everything else.

● You rarely see immediate results of your work. Youth work is a "sower" type of ministry. Planting seeds that may come to blossom years later is part of the job description.

● Young people are, by nature, a more difficult group to reach. While adults are able to maintain a facade of interest, young people let you know how they're thinking and feeling. They are unpredictable, acting different ways at different times. They desperately need you to help them through this transition. But you may never know it.

On top of these built-in youth ministry frustrations, there are the ones youth leaders bring upon themselves. They may have hidden agendas about what they would like to see happen. For example, a youth leader complained that things moved too slowly. Some probing revealed that he wanted to have things changed in time for his graduation from seminary. He had set a goal, but it wasn't the group's, nor the church's.

Perhaps the most common frustrations come from lack of deliberate, detail-oriented planning. Putting things off is one kind of planning—the kind most likely to breed frustration. Finally, the greatest frustration is having no one with whom to share life's thorns.

SOME SOLUTIONS

Moses was a great leader who knew God in a special way. They talked directly to one another. Moses even felt free to get angry at God, knowing that God could take it. What was God's solution to Moses' frustration? God to Moses: "Assemble 70 respected men ... and I will take some of the spirit I have given you and give it to them. Then they can help you bear the responsibility for these people, and you will not have to bear it alone" (Numbers 11:16-17).

Essentially, God told Moses to stop being a Lone Ranger. Of course, Moses had to change roles. Formerly, Moses took all the responsibility (and glory). Now, he would have to train and coordinate a group of helpers, who'd also serve as his support group. And it worked. How can we use Moses as a youth minister model?

● First, go to God with your frustrations. Tell him how you're feeling. Ask him for guidance. After praying, you should not only feel better, but your head will be ready for thinking out your problem.

● Seek the advice of peers. A support group is necessary for your health. This support group should be composed of adults who listen and care. You need more than the kids in

Beating the 'Moses Syndrome'

All youth leaders, whether paid or volunteer, have at one time or another experienced a feeling of inadequacy in ministry. I call this the "Moses Syndrome," based on Exodus 6:30 in which Moses pleaded with God about his lack of eloquent speech; Moses' excuse was a result of an inadequate self-image.

There are basically four things which can make you feel inadequate in youth ministry, but each can be overcome:

Parents, who often have more experience raising and training youth than you do. They may have the "What makes you so qualified?" attitude.

You are on the same side as the parents, but you play a different role. Youth may go to you with some problems that they wouldn't take to their parents; you play an important part in your young people's spiritual development.

Build up parents in the eyes of the youth. Let the parents know you are backing them up.

An experienced pastor, who may have so many great ideas and plans that you feel creatively inferior.

Learn from the pastor's suggestions. Modify those pointers, using your own God-given creativity. Add new spice to old ideas and make them relevant for today's young people.

Spiritual shortcomings, when you wonder, "How can I teach others when my own life isn't totally together?"

All people in youth leadership fight spiritual battles. That's not the issue. The issue is does God want you in youth work? If so, then stop being discouraged about your shortcomings and concentrate on the job God wants you to do.

Age, when you hear older leaders talk about past experiences and you can't even find a personal illustration to introduce your first church youth night sermon.

It's not your physical age that matters, though, it's your spiritual maturity (see 1 Timothy 4:12). People won't look so much at your age if they see a real devotion to God.

—Tom Franks

your group to feed your own needs. Seek the counsel and support of leaders in other churches. Push back your pride. Be transparent. No one can help unless you communicate your honest feelings. Good support groups help you realize that the weight of the world isn't on your shoulders alone. They may even help you laugh and take yourself less seriously.

● Sort out the reasons for your frustrations. What were your expectations? Were they too high? If so, what are realistic expectations? If your expectations were fair, what blocked your endeavor? Can these blocks be overcome? List those reasons on paper. Then evaluate them.

● Deal with the feelings generated by frustration. Some of these feelings are anger, hurt, loss and sadness. Admit that you have these feelings and get them out. Spend time with a trusted friend and support group members. Go jogging, swimming, or to a gym and punch a bag. Do anything that ventilates the feelings but doesn't hurt anybody.

● Displace some of your responsibility. Moses gave away some of his responsibility. Give away some of yours. Ask young people to share in the responsibility. You may need to call them on Thursday, Friday and Saturday to make sure something will happen on Sunday. Other adults will need encouragement and fresh ideas as they carry some of the responsibilities.

The benefits of shared leadership are positive. Your youth will learn leadership skills. Because everything doesn't depend on you, success and failure become group experiences.

● Take caution in sharing your frustration with the youth. If the youth are directly related to the problem, then share your frustration. For example, if you've worked for a year with a group and there appears to have been little spiritual growth, share your frustration with the youth. This will be an invitation for them to help you work through a problem that relates directly to them. However, if the frustration is not directly related to them, don't spread problems. For instance, don't let the group in on the friction between you and the senior pastor. It's your hassle, not theirs.

● Love for your kids is your best friend. Your Christian love for the youth can help you overcome your frustrations. If you see youth ministry as a first-class endeavor, then it matters less if others rank it second-class. Your love for young people will enable you to understand their half-adult/half-child personalities. You'll enjoy seeing them change and grow. You'll share their accomplishments, no matter how small they may seem to others. And you'll help them through hurts as an adult who cares. You'll stand by them even if you see no changes.

Finally, you can be satisfied with doing your best, even if it seems you're the only one who will ever know. Moses never saw the fruit of the seeds he planted. He couldn't enter into the Promised Land. Yet he stayed with a frustrating task, keeping his first priority of being faithful to God. As youth workers, we need to see above the frustrating day-to-day problems and realize that we are part of God's plan to bring humanity to Christ, the new Promised Land. In light of the big picture, our frustrations fall to the proper place.

ADDITIONAL READING

The Basic Encyclopedia for Youth Ministry, Dennis C. Benson and Bill Wolfe, Group Books.

Managing Our Work, John W. Alexander, InterVarsity.

Your supervisor's support isn't automatic. An experienced pastor tells how to earn and develop it.

You Can Earn and Develop Supervisor Support

BY RUSS RITCHEL

"**I**'m not getting the support I need." Bill's reason for leaving his staff position after only two years was brief and to the point. How many times have you heard this complaint from workers in your church? How many times have you said it to yourself?

Bill's comment stood out because he couldn't answer my simple follow-up question, "How did you help your supervisor support you?" He floundered. For Bill, support was a one-way street; it was his superior's responsibility. Bill felt he only needed to do a good job.

Support is a commodity that everyone expects. But few of us actually cultivate this precious dimension of staff relationships. Being on both ends of this supervisor/supervisee relationship has helped me to understand specific actions which send distinct support/non-support messages to supervisors.

There are several things you can do to show your superiors that you want and deserve their support.

MINIMIZE SURPRISES

Most supervisors don't like surprises, especially unpleasant ones. But the natural inclination is to cover up mistakes and conflicts, unknowingly leaving someone else to tell our supervisor about them. Yet, thirdhand news is usually distorted. If you're at fault, you should be the person to break the news—in private. It may mean swallowing your pride, but the price is worth it.

Once I was faced with a tough situation at a retreat. Late Saturday, three junior high boys were caught with drugs and a half-bottle of whiskey. Because our expectation list said such cases would result in being sent home, we had little choice. I imagined the boys' parents getting upset and cornering the pastor (my supervisor, who'd be unaware of the problem) in the church lobby the next morning. I phoned him late that night. I wanted to keep him informed.

In case of any doubt, try to inform anyone who might be affected, regardless of the situation.

COMMUNICATE

Communicate your plans to your superior. Little things often make a great difference. Our pastor receives a copy of every youth mailing. We make an appointment to tell him what happened at each major event. It's important that you make the appointment. It says "I want you to know" instead of giving the impression that your superior has to infiltrate your ministry to find out what is going on. Periodic meetings when there have been no major events keep your supervisor informed if anyone asks him or her about something you're planning.

FIT THE FLOW

Create an atmosphere of continuity. I always check my direction to make sure that it fits the church's flow. This process should begin with the job interview. Before accepting a youth ministry position, take stock of the direction—spiritually and programmatically—the church is headed. Whether your direction and style can fit in may determine whether you belong in that ministry. No senior minister should have to lie awake nights wondering if the staff members are pursuing the same goals. If you're already a staff member, you should ask yourself, "Am I here to build the kingdom of God under this pastor's leadership or am I looking to build my own little kingdom in the midst of this church?" If the latter is the case, maybe you should consider employment elsewhere.

Fitting your church's flow involves active listening. Supervisors set a program's direction. Even if you have no written guidelines or goals, you can quickly determine much through regular contact with your superior.

On returning from a trip, I was greeted with a report of an emergency in my department. The person I left in charge said to me, "This is the way I handled it; it's not what I would have done, but it is what I thought you would have done." You can imagine the confidence I had the next time I left things in his hands! His listening was active. He understood our differences in style. He supported my leadership. I am not suggesting that you must compromise principles. In a supportive relationship, nine out of 10 conflicts in style and direction can be resolved without any compromise in the basics of ministry.

QUESTION

It is nearly impossible to give all the details of a project on the first try. In addition, situations arise which raise questions requiring your supervisor's input. Quick contacts and midcourse corrections save a lot of agony when a project is finished. "I just wanted to make sure I've caught what you had in mind," is a sentence which is music to most supervisors' ears. Not to ask these questions puts your supervisor in a nightmarish position of making sure he or she has given you every detail the first time through. Questions are not a sign of ineptitude, but of a sincere desire to please and fit in.

SUPPORT

The final suggestion is obvious. If you want support, you need to first support your boss. Nothing does more to destroy relationships than having your superiors hear that you told five people what you think is wrong with them. When word gets out that you have complaints, you will become a magnet for complainers. You'll become the focal point for most of the malcontents in the church.

Most pastors know when a staff member complains. Who

can trust a subordinate who criticizes constantly? The person cultivating support will most often keep tight rein on his or her conversation.

Nearly every supervisor who wants to keep a staff member will support him or her. However, support is a shared responsibility. Some pastors genuinely want to support their staff, but look in vain for areas in which they feel on solid ground. Make your support as much earned as it is expected.

ADDITIONAL READING

Enlist, Train, Support Church Leaders, Evelyn Huber, Judson.

The Ministry of Management, Stephen Douglass, Bruce Cook and Howard Hendricks, Here's Life.

Relationships can be a vital
source of renewal. Support
systems don't always 'happen,' we often need to cultivate them.

CHAPTER 20

How to Build A Support System

BY JOANI SCHULTZ

● "It usually comes in the middle of a youth retreat when all the kids are going different directions. I feel so out of control. That's when I need support."

● "My pastor's an alcoholic. He's also a pillar of our community. Who can I confide in when I know he's been drinking?"

● "I can't help but feel guilty. I'm supposed to be the 'expert' in relationships—but my husband and I are getting a divorce. I need someone I can trust with the news of my crumbling marriage."

● "Ever since I came to this church, I've been alone. I might as well be on a deserted island. There's nobody to talk to. Nobody cares."

Everyone needs support. No one enjoys being alone and isolated from love. Youth leaders—like everyone else—need support.

For those of us who spend our lives ministering and giving to teenagers, support systems become our battery-chargers. Receiving support revitalizes and energizes so we can keep on going.

But switching from the role of helping others with relationships to building relationships ourselves is sometimes difficult. Instead of being the constant "giver," we need to occasionally become the "taker." This "taking" happens through another's empathetic ear, continual encouragement, and confrontations when necessary.

Some say support systems "just happen." Margaret Rickers, a 10-year youth ministry veteran from Colorado, says: "Support is an invisible kind of thing. You usually don't identify people as a 'support system'—you just know."

Yet there are others who don't consider support so spontaneous. "Support doesn't 'just happen,' " remarks Liz Spence, a United Methodist pastor. "You've got to create situations and the tools to make it happen."

Support. Even if it is invisible, it's real. And it's ultimately necessary for you, as a leader, to have the energy and encouragement to be the best possible minister you can be. Building a support system is worth the effort.

THE SOURCES OF SUPPORT

So, how do youth leaders get surrounded by comforting, caring people? It happens differently for different people. Support systems vary as widely as the places and people involved. Each approach differs from person to person, situation to situation.

Following are a number of leaders' answers to the question, "Where does support come from?" Sift through these true stories. See what has and hasn't worked. Learn from these models of support and consider how to adapt them to meet your needs.

Can support come from my senior pastor? Because every situation is unique, it's difficult to offer a hard and fast rule concerning your senior pastor's support.

Pat Jeffrey, an associate pastor from Kansas, responds: "Getting support is a real stickler for me. It's difficult. I wish I could turn to my senior pastor, but in both congregations I've been in, it's seldom happened. So our church formed a personnel committee that meets with me quarterly."

One youth worker from Virginia, Tim Taylor, relates: "I get support from my senior pastor when I hit rough spots.

Whenever a parent or youth complains, my senior pastor brings the information back to me in a positive way. He cares about me and allows me the freedom to handle the situation on my own. Communication is open because we meet weekly."

Vicky Camp, a lay volunteer for 10 years from Illinois, says: "We work with another couple and laugh about the things that happen with the kids. They're so much help. But I know we could go to the pastor for support and I feel strongly we'd get it. We've never had to do that yet—but I'm sure we'd get his support."

Is support found inside or outside the congregation?
The question of "inside or outside" depends largely on the circumstances involved. It's best to build a strong foundation of members who'll support you when the going gets rough. But when a situation hits too close to home and congregational members can no longer be objective, it's time to look elsewhere.

"The time I needed support in the congregation had to do with the choir I was directing," says a youth leader from Alabama. "A few people, who thought they 'ruled,' didn't like the kind of music I chose." Since this was an internal problem in the congregation, the youth and music director felt the need to seek support outside the congregation. "I needed someone to look at things objectively, so I went to a pastor outside the congregation to be my friend. I feel you really can't go to someone 'in' the congregation and expect them to be objective."

There are others whose situations contrast that example. Leslie Petit, director of youth and Christian education ministries, says she wouldn't have taken the job at her California church if the congregation hadn't "bought into" the idea of support. In fact, the congregation formed a "youth ministry team" whose sole function was to be supportive. "There are times when I'm burnt out—especially when it comes to church politics. But my youth ministry team (made up of youth and adults) naturally takes over and becomes a good support."

A New Mexico pastor adds: "The key to my support system is my willingness to be vulnerable and take risks. I need people to minister to me." As a pastor who's recently gone through a divorce, she continues: "I was willing to let them (the congregation) know about my divorce early on. Publicly I asked them to support and love me—even if they didn't agree with me. My openness made my painful situation a healthier one." Looking back at the marriage breakup, she appreciates the solid foundation of relationships previously established. "The total congregation became my family. My entire ministry has been intentional about listening and caring. And the congregation was willing to listen."

In a similar situation, a congregational member told his youth minister: "All these years you've listened and supported us. Now it's our turn to do the same for you."

When given the opportunity, the church, the family of God, can minister and support leaders in incredible ways.

Can other youth leaders be a support? Confiding in coworkers, those who share the same job in other places, furnishes an empathetic avenue for sharing failures and successes. Because of "like" ministries, youth leaders are bound together by a special kind of understanding.

Yet one group of youth leaders met for support and their meetings turned into a subtle game of "Can you top this one?" After a while, some members dreaded going because their own youth ministry programs weren't flashy and flamboyant, kids did drop out, creative ideas didn't flow naturally.

However, one youth minister went to such meetings seeking the excellent support that can be found with peers. The trouble was, he began feeling whenever he shared his dilemmas, he brought a negative tone to the meetings. Soon he didn't want to control the peer get-togethers by filling conversations with his church's war stories.

Both illustrations suggest imbalance. But it is possible to foster a healthy sharing, of the "goods" and "bads," which creates a beautiful stronghold for leaders. Begin by building trust and camaraderie so members don't feel a need to "impress" or "depress" each other.

Can my spouse be a support? What if you're married? What role does your spouse play in the whole support-system scheme? Is it fair to demand one person's constant support? Or is that what God intended for marriage? Responses differ.

Lewis Graydon, director of youth and education from Alabama, declares: "My spouse is my best support person. But I consider the two of us one person. When I share things with her, it's like not telling anyone."

Youth worker Tim Taylor adds: "I can react and say things to my wife that I wouldn't say in public. She's my sounding board. She always brings me back to reality."

To make the most of a marriage support system, one leader deliberately makes dates with his wife. Also, every morning they share in a devotion time.

Does professional help provide a support system? But what happens if your senior pastor fails to respond, your congregation is oblivious to your needs, and friends are miles away? When circumstances reach the boiling point, consider reaching out for professional help.

"I'd been looking for people in the congregation who would work 'with' me. But no. There wasn't anybody I felt I could talk to. So I figured something must be wrong with me. It got to be so bad that whenever things got tense, I'd get migraine headaches. Emotionally and physically, I couldn't go on."

That's the story of one full-time professional youth minister in a Minnesota church. Wearing the demanding hats of youth worker, husband, and father of five was too much. Unbearable headaches, strain on the family and an "I'm-at-fault" attitude led him to seek professional help. Through the support and therapy of a psychologist, he gradually learned to cope.

Whenever situations expand to dangerous proportions, or even if you just need someone to talk with, get help. Professional counseling provides an objective listener who's trained to do just that.

Don't view professional help as a sign of weakness. On the contrary, recognizing your need for support and direction is a strength. It's been said that someone who seeks professional help is actually seeking a friend, and needing a friend is part of being human.

TOOLS FOR BUILDING YOUR SUPPORT SYSTEM

Building support doesn't start with the people around you, it begins with you. Your openness and initiative bring support into being. Here are tools to make support happen for you:

Admit you need support—One struggling pastor said: "I

need people to minister to me. That means I've got to be willing to tell people I don't have it all together." How can you grow and learn if you don't allow yourself the freedom to recognize you can't do it alone?

God's creative plan revolves around the working, functioning idea that "Christ is like a single body, which has many

---

FIND THE RIGHT SUPPORT PEOPLE

In hunting for the "right" type of person to support you, look for someone with these qualities:

● **Objectivity**—A friend who remains open and doesn't take sides is invaluable. If someone's "too close" to the situation, objectivity diminishes.

● **Listening ear**—A treasured support person doesn't give advice. Even when you "beg" for someone to tell you what to do, a listener listens, supports and encourages, but allows you freedom to decide for yourself.

● **Focus on yourself**—When you're hurting, confide in people who'll center their attention on your needs. Beware of the person who brushes your needs aside by saying: "I know how you feel. I remember when *I* . . ." or, "Yes, that's like the time *I* . . ." The attention turns to the other person instead of you at a time when you need consolation.

● **Truthful**—"What I need is someone to tell me the truth about me," commented one leader. "Love me enough to risk our love. If I'm wrong, crabby or negative, I need a friend to tell me. That's the greatest love: Telling me things I might not want to hear, but are true." Finding someone who'll be willing to love you enough to be truly honest is a remarkable and rare gift. In his book **The Road Less Traveled**, Dr. M. Scott Peck states, "For the truly loving person, the act of criticism or confrontation does not come easily."

● **Faith-centered**—Seek a person who focuses on God's wisdom and overall plan. Treasure the friendships that are glued with the common bond of Christianity. With faith motivating your support people, God's loving touch will be there.

parts; it is still one body, even though it is made up of different parts" (1 Corinthians 12:12).

Realize your vulnerability—Digest Paul's words: "When I am weak, then I am strong" (2 Corinthians 12:10b). Displaying weakness or needs to a trusted friend, a local congregation or a professional therapist indicates a sign of strength. Being vulnerable demonstrates your willingness to become a better person.

Take a risk—"Building a support system is often a method of trial and error. It begins each time we learn to reach out," says one youth leader from New Mexico. "I'm intuitive now about taking relational risks, but that's come from a lot of trial and tribulation. Even if I'm burned 20 or 30 times, I don't give up on trying to make friends." This person knows the potential hurt and help found through risk-taking. Maybe risk-taking is one more way of understanding Jesus' words, "No, not seven times—but seventy times seven" (Matthew 18:22).

Take the initiative—Find one person, or more. Then make the first move. Don't be afraid of joining activities outside the church. One youth leader from Colorado reports: "I go to things where I can meet people. I've attended singles meetings, met with other youth directors in the community, joined a guild and a health club." Expand your contacts by making the first move.

Seek a variety of people—Leaders possess many needs. There are those who say, "Find support people who are going through the same kinds of things." Others add, "I choose other people to support me—those who don't have a specific interest in youth ministry."

Leslie Petit advises: "It's a necessity to have many different kinds of people. If they're all the same, it's not as advantageous as different people."

Lee McGlasson, a youth pastor from California, says: "If I look only to my peers in similar circumstances, they'll have similar feelings. But other people's age and their economic status bring a different perspective. What I might see as a threatening situation, others may see as a challenge."

Schedule support—The more you cherish support, the more you'll incorporate it into your schedule. Some youth leader friends meet for lunch every four to six weeks to discuss youth ministry issues and cultivate their relationships.

One group of leaders meets weekly for a Bible study which rotates leadership responsibility for the discussion.

Reflect on past support people—Lee McGlasson remembers: "When I was going through a really rough time, Walt would take me to my favorite restaurant. He'd help me 'see around the corner' and remember how God had pulled me through in the past. You know, at the time he was helping me, I didn't even realize it. I look back and see those as precious moments."

Tim Taylor reflects on a couple in his congregation: "When I first came, I got discouraged. But they were always by my side. They didn't judge or condemn me. Looking back, I realize they were instrumental in helping me through the first years of my ministry."

So live by faith—not by sight. "To have faith is to be sure of the things we hope for, to be certain of the things we cannot see" (Hebrews 11:1). In the midst of troubled times, you might be blind to the fact that people are supporting you now. To help you see that, remember special friends from your past.

Be patient—Supportive relationships take time. Again, unique circumstances and personalities determine how "fast" a support person is gained. For some it begins as quickly as a conference retreat weekend with peers. For others the process is prolonged. Tim Taylor enjoys deep friendships with young people from his congregation. But he notes: "It takes more than a year or two to build relationships. To me, my close support group began after being here four years. I say, 'Don't get discouraged.' "

Lewis Graydon adds: "It took me a year to find one person. And that took a lot of praying and seeking the Lord's guidance."

Remember God—In spite of a youth worker's loyalty and commitment to faith, it's possible to slip away from personal prayer, Bible study and worship. Do your best to remain close to the Word. When times get rough, God is forever whispering, "I am with you always."

And God creatively continues to touch lives through people. Theologian Martin Marty once remarked: "What a friend we have in Jesus. What a Jesus we have in a friend."

Your church should include
youth ministry in its annual
budget. This chapter tells
you how to get formal
funding for your ministry.

CHAPTER
21

How to Land
Church Funds
For Youth Ministry

BY RICH BIMLER

I remember hearing a church leader proudly announce
that his church had budgeted $50 for youth for the com-
ing year. And he was even prouder when the church didn't
spend it all during the entire year.

Let me say it from the start: A church's financial involvement in youth ministry is usually in direct proportion to its
youth ministry's effectiveness. A church's financial support
of its youth ministry is generally an indicator of how much
the adults care about their youth.

Instead of encouraging young people to sponsor bake
sales, car washes, slave days and other fund-raising projects, it is better to make sure that youth ministry is a specific entry in the congregational budget each year.

Recognizing youth ministry as a budget item promotes the
idea that youth ministry is a vital and strategic part of the
total church's ministry, on par with the elders, Sunday
school, evangelism committee and worship. By excluding
youth ministry in a church's budget, that congregation says

that youth and youth ministry are merely "extra" or "sub" parts of their work.

Now, before you burn all the cookies intended for the bake sale or turn off the faucets for the car wash, understand that certain fund-raising projects can be healthy and meaningful for youth and youth groups (but not to support your church's regular ministry with youth). Instead, special projects are helpful for special causes such as:

● raising money for hunger projects.

● sponsoring refugee teenagers to attend a youth conference.

● buying a new pingpong table for the youth room.

● funding a special party.

● traveling to a national youth conference.

Fund-raising projects help develop a close-knit group of youth and adults as they work together toward a common goal. Projects provide a way for good team- and community-building.

But, as stated before, youth group fund raisers shouldn't be the sole means of finances. Encouraging your congregation to include youth ministry as a regular expenditure in your church budget will:

● help your church understand that youth ministry is an integral and vital part of your total ministry.

● promote the concept that youth ministry is not just the youth group, but *all* the ways young people are involved in ministry.

● involve your young people in your congregation's decision-making process. If youth ministry is to be funded through your church, young people should be involved in developing the budget, not only on youth ministry items, but in other ministry areas as well.

● encourage young people to give their offerings to the Lord through the Sunday morning worship, rather than dissecting that offering from what they may give to the youth group or other youth projects. Young people should be involved in the total stewardship effort of their congregation.

● become another way for youth and adults to work together, getting better acquainted with each other so that ministry happens.

If your church doesn't include funding for youth ministry in your annual budget, how can you encourage them to do so? Here are 10 tested approaches:

1. **Begin slowly.** The first step is to get youth ministry included in the budget. Don't be too concerned with the total amount, at least for the first year.

2. **Be an advocate** for youth ministry by sharing your feelings with people in decision-making positions. Talk individually with them, rather than bringing this idea up "cold" at the next assembly or board meeting.

3. **Stress the importance** of young people being genuine and regular parts of the church's total ministry program.

4. **Encourage** young people to speak about their thoughts and support of this approach.

5. **Stress** that including youth ministry as a regular part of the church's budget will help to increase young people's stewardship involvement in the church.

6. **Be concerned** about ways in which the needs of other age groups are reflected in the church budget. For example, perhaps the elderly also are "left out" in terms of specific ways to meet their needs through financial resources. Maybe their group can be your next budget priority. But work on one budget area at a time.

7. **Discuss your feelings** with your professional church staff to get their support and to eliminate any surprises for them.

8. **Encourage** all young people to get offering envelopes (if your church uses them) so that they can contribute regularly to the church's ministry.

9. **If you need** to increase the amount of financial resources available for youth ministry, prepare a proposed youth ministry budget, begin to get approval for it from your pastoral staff and various boards, and keep it in line with the total needs of your church. Then present it as a realistic way to continue the development of youth ministry.

10. **Compare** what other churches in your area have for youth ministry resources. Learn from each other.

A youth ministry budget is a basic tool for effective youth ministry. It helps youth and adults to better sense that they are the church of today working together in ministry with each other. A youth ministry budget is much more than simple figures. It is a mind-set and style of youth ministry that is effective, positive and essential for youth ministry to meet the needs of young people.

TWO YOUTH MINISTRY BUDGETS

Depending on the size of the congregation, amounts included for youth ministry will vary a great deal. Here are models of youth ministry budgets from two congregations of different sizes.

Church No. 1: Three hundred members, small town, 30 high school youth, 20 junior highers, no one knows how many young adults.

1. Resource materials for adult workers with youth (magazines, books) .... $ 100.00
2. Resource materials for youth officers 50.00
3. Equipment and supplies 100.00
4. Conferences and training events for adult workers.......... 250.00
5. Conferences and training events for youth leaders 200.00
6. Guest speakers 150.00
7. Growth and planning retreats 150.00
8. Special events....................................... 100.00
9. Miscellaneous....................................... 100.00

$1,200.00

Church No. 2: More than 1,800 members, 300 youth, 150 junior highers, 85 young adults, one full-time youth minister.

1. Salary, benefits..................................... $25,000.00
2. Youth ministry library and resource materials 500.00
3. Youth room supplies 250.00
4. Resource materials for leaders 500.00
5. Training for youth counselors 500.00
6. Materials and equipment for youth ministry board 500.00
7. Conference and seminar tuition grants 500.00
8. Youth scholarships to training events 500.00
9. Church work scholarships 2,500.00
10. Planning retreats 600.00
11. Youth trip and district events 500.00
12. Equipment and supplies 300.00
13. Guest speakers 350.00
14. Supplies for interest groups (music, drama, band, athletics).. 500.00
15. Miscellaneous..................................... 250.00

$33,250.00

ADDITIONAL READING

A New Start in Youth Ministry, Leo Symmank and Eldor Kaiser, Concordia.

Developing youth ministry
interns is a major under-
taking. But the rewards can
be great for all involved.

CHAPTER

22

Youth Ministry Apprentices

BY JIM HANCOCK

Rob, a pastor at a small church, has been asked a question he's never before considered: What *would* he do with a youth ministry intern?

After several minutes, Rob answers that he would:

- help the intern avoid some of the mistakes he made,
- teach a philosophy of youth ministry,
- expand his own effectiveness through the intern's additional help,
- give the intern responsibility for some of the on-campus ministry,
- and let the intern have the junior high kids.

Of course, all this is just speculation. Rob doubts that an internship could work in his situation because his church is:

- too small,
- too set in its ways,
- too tight with its money,
- not very committed to youth work,
- and not greatly excited about interns.

Still, the notion intrigues him. Rob begins asking questions.

Question No. 1:
WHAT DOES MY CHURCH HAVE TO OFFER AN INTERN?

An intern is not just cheap labor. Nor is he or she another volunteer. An intern is a student—an apprentice. Understanding that special relationship affects what you offer an intern in responsibility, salary and training.

The first step in developing a positive intern experience is to consider what your church *can* offer.

Begin by devising a schedule of youth ministry reading and accompanying discussion sessions. Plan to teach such skills and theory as message and Bible study preparation, time management and scheduling, and small and large group dynamics. Plan to expose your intern to important resource people in your congregation and community: counseling professionals, gifted preachers, talented Bible teachers, successful managers and other youth workers.

Plan to delegate responsibility and authority carefully. Don't forget to evaluate performance and progress frequently enough to help the intern grow by your reinforcement and correction.

Numerous factors influence an intern's salary. Whatever the salary, the guiding principle should be to at least meet the intern's basic needs. Don't forget the incidental expenses your intern will incur in the course of working with kids.

An internship is not an occupation; it's a stepping stone to something more. You can offer an intern a realistic look at youth ministry. The time the intern spends with you, watching you model the ministry, listening to you answer the question, "We do it this way because . . ." will probably turn out to be the heart of the curriculum. You may launch someone into a career in youth work. Or, you may save someone from disappointment and failure in a career that is wrong for him or her.

Question No. 2:
WHAT CAN I EXPECT FROM AN INTERN?

With rare exceptions, interns produce the work of, well, interns. They are in the learning process and will take uncertain and wrong steps at times. Your intern will look to you for direction.

Give your intern a thorough job description which includes responsibilities, hours, relationships and expectations. The less you leave to assumptions, the fewer surprises for either of you. Before hiring an intern be sure as much as possible that he or she fits the job. It's easier to not hire than to fire.

Your job description should include:
- who will be the supervisor
- purpose of the position
- approximate weekly hours
- specific responsibilities
- opportunities
- expectations
- evaluation criteria and procedure

Give a written evaluation of performance and progress in each area of the job description at least once during the internship.

Question No. 3:
HOW LONG SHOULD AN INTERNSHIP LAST?

Internships can range from one summer to 15 months. The merits of various lengths of time vary.

Summertime internships add personnel reinforcements during the heaviest youth ministry season of the year. Kids are out of school and bored, programming is often more frequent and varied.

But summer is also the time when you are least able to supervise an intern. The likelihood of problems is greater because your attention is divided.

A nine-month or year-long program allows the intern to benefit more from contact with his or her supervisor. The youth group gains from an intern's presence through an entire school year. Furthermore, the unfolding of a whole year of ministry can be invaluable to the intern.

The 15-month program maximizes the combination of the summer and year-long internships by including two summers in the program. The first summer prepares the intern for a more productive second summer.

However, the lengthier the internship, the greater the dollar cost. Longer internships also limit the types of people who can fill the position. Only someone who is a local student, has a flexible job schedule, or is willing to take an extended leave from his or her present activities can consider such a program.

In any case, it's probably better to take on a 10- to 12-week intern during the summer than it is to plunge into a 15-month commitment.

Question No. 4:
WHAT KIND OF PERSON MAKES A GOOD INTERN?

The qualifications for an intern are not unlike those for a good volunteer: personal and spiritual maturity, pure motivation, love for kids, flexibility, commitment and team orientation. Look for someone who is considering a career in ministry. The internship is often a part of the process which confirms (and occasionally denies) the leaning toward a ministry related career.

Question No. 5:
WHERE DO WE LOOK FOR SUCH A PERSON?

Frequently, the best interns are found among those who have grown up within your own church. Interns reared in your area can exhibit the most sensitivity to the needs of your youth.

Next, look to Christian colleges and seminaries. Most will have a placement officer who will be delighted to post your job notice, description and application for the students. Look especially to the handful of schools with majors or minors in youth ministry.

Let your friends in youth ministry know about the program. Spread the word in the lay community, especially among single adults.

More than anything, pray.

Question No. 6:
ARE INTERNS REALLY WORTH IT?

You bet they are! In nearly a decade of internships at our church, we have gotten better at making it worth our while. At this writing, we have three year-round interns working part time (two with senior high and one with junior high.) Two are students at a local college and the third also works part time for InterVarsity Christian Fellowship.

Over half the interns we've employed have continued on

to ministry careers. We've not only helped our youth program and the interns involved, but the church too.

We're always experimenting with new ways of working with interns. Of course, there have been marginally successful experiences, even failures. But, we're glad to have an intern program and have every intention of continuing and improving it.

BACK TO ROB

No one can sell Rob an intern-training package for his church that guarantees success. But Rob's research has given him greater hope for the potentials of an internship in his church.

What remains is to complete the necessary homework and sell the idea to his supervisor and the rest of the church. Then, if he gets that far, develop an effective intern program. He's a long way from welcoming his first intern; however, good things don't happen overnight.

ADDITIONAL READING

Volunteer Youth Workers: Recruiting and Developing Leaders for Youth Ministry, J. David Stone and Rose Mary Miller, Group Books.

Youth Ministry: The New Team Approach, Ginny Ward Holderness, John Knox.

It's important to evaluate
our ministries. This Bible
study helps us clarify
what's happening in our
lives and to seek God's
direction.

CHAPTER

23

When Things
Fall Apart—
A Bible Study

BY JOANI SCHULTZ

"**W**hen Things Fall Apart" is for those who work
with young people—youth sponsors, youth directors, pastors, high school Bible class teachers and other
adult volunteers who've made a commitment to youth
ministry.

Your church might have just you or two or 20 who have
made that commitment. Whatever the number, you can creatively bring this Bible study to life in a variety of ways. Use
this study for:

● individual study and personal reflection.
● youth sponsors. (It's best if the group is small. Six to
eight people is a good, workable number.)
● your core of leaders—both youth and adults.
● teachers who work with the high school Bible class.
● an appreciation time or wrap-up for those who've
worked with youth during the past year.

WHY A BIBLE STUDY FOR LEADERS?

Youth ministry can be discouraging. Activities don't go the

way we plan. Three kids show up for a meeting when we expected 20. Joe drops out of Bible class. Shelly runs away from home in spite of counseling.

Maintaining a proper perspective in our ministries is a challenge. It's important to evaluate what we do, look objectively at circumstances and discover God's purpose in our lives.

Youth ministry involves faith in God and in the abilities he's given us. Paul's second letter to the Corinthians offers timely words that speak to us—we are special people who have been given a special message.

Objective. To help leaders realize their role as "clay pots" that God uses to share his message.

Leaders will:

- tell about frustrations and joys youth ministry brings.
- look for God's action in struggles and difficult times.
- celebrate the hope we have because of God's power.

Supplies. Bibles, construction paper, scissors, tape, pencils or markers. (Optional: a list of your congregation's young people, a small pottery gift for each participant.)

WHAT TO DO

1. Ask the participants to tear or cut construction paper into the shape of a clay pot. Encourage them to create shapes that represent how they feel about their involvement in youth ministry.

2. Instruct them to write their first names on the top of their clay pots and share their reasons for the shapes.

3. Read 2 Corinthians 4:8-9. The verses illustrate four feelings of discouragement followed by words of hope. Instruct the participants to rip their pots into four sections and write portions of each verse on the front and back of the individual pot pieces such as:

front of piece one—"often troubled"

front of piece two—"sometimes in doubt"

front of piece three—"many enemies"

front of piece four—"badly hurt at times"

back of piece one—"but not crushed"

back of piece two—"but never in despair"

back of piece three—"but never without a friend"

back of piece four—"but not destroyed"

4. Ask each person to look at the front and back of each torn piece and think of a time when he or she felt those feelings. Have everyone write the situations on the appropriate piece. For example: "I felt doubt when I talked with Jill and she made fun of church and the youth group. But I wasn't in despair because I prayed for her and trusted God would work in her life. Yesterday she asked what the youth group was doing."

5. Encourage participants to fill in as many pieces as possible. Each time or situation should relate to their personal experiences in youth ministry. Invite each person to share at least two experiences with the group.

6. Have participants read 2 Corinthians 4:1-18 silently and each choose one verse that's especially meaningful concerning youth ministry; share responses with the group.

PIECING IT ALL TOGETHER

Discuss the following questions with the entire group:

2 Corinthians 4:1—What keeps you from being discouraged? What do you do when you are discouraged? How is working with young people encouraging? How can it be discouraging? To bolster your spirit, read Romans 8:16-17, 28, 38-39. What do you think is the secret of avoiding discouragement?

2 Corinthians 4:4—When young people fail to respond to the gospel, what's the reason? Is it important or necessary to "blame" the evil god of this world? Why or why not? What does 1 Peter 5:8-9 add? Does that change your approach to youth ministry? Explain. If your youth ministry is struggling, is someone or something at "fault"? Explain.

2 Corinthians 4:5—How can this verse represent the core of youth ministry? In youth ministry, how can you tell when Jesus is in or out of focus? What impact does this verse have on your efforts? If you're preaching "yourself," how do you know? What danger signs point to that? Read Matthew 5:14-16 and share how you think it relates to this verse in 2 Corinthians.

2 Corinthians 4:7—How does it feel to be described as a clay pot? What images do you see when you think of yourself as the clay and God as the potter? Read Isaiah 45:9-10; 64:8; Romans 9:20-21. How do these verses add to that imagery? Why is it important to believe that supreme power belongs to God? What advice would you give someone who's beginning to work with young people?

2 Corinthians 4:18—Think of one young person that you feel especially good about and tell why. Now think of someone whom you worry about and have a deep concern for. Tell why. What's the difference between the two young people? How does this verse offer hope for both kids? What relationship does faith have to youth ministry? Read 2 Corinthians 5:7 and Hebrews 11:1.

When everyone has had an opportunity to share, return each construction-paper pot to the person who designed it. Distribute the tape and tell everyone to piece the pots back together. Talk about what "holds" adults together in youth ministry.

PRAYER OPTIONS

● Exchange clay pots and invite each person to pray for the person named on the pot he or she received. Have participants take the clay pots home as reminders to pray for the individual throughout the week.

● Encourage each adult to think of one young person in your church and pray for him or her.

● Compile a list of your church's young people. Divide the list among the study participants. Encourage them to pray for one young person on the list each day.

● As a gift of appreciation and a reminder that we are "clay pots," give each participant a small clay pot. Fill it with the names of young people in your congregation. Encourage adults to draw a name from the jar each week and pray for that person.

PERSONAL DEVOTIONS

Read these verses when you feel as if things are falling apart: Psalms 25:4-5; 27:1; 50:15; 62:1-12; 121:1-2

Ecclesiastes 3:1-8

Read these verses when you feel things are finally coming together: Psalms 8:1—9:2; 30:4-5; 118:5-9

1 Corinthians 1:3-4

Ephesians 1:19-20; 3:16-21

Philippians 2:1-11

1 Thessalonians 5:16-18

Having trouble living with the levels of authority in your church? These servant-style approaches can bring new life to you and your ministry.

CHAPTER 24

Handling The Reality Of Being No. 2

BY JOANI SCHULTZ

DO ANY OF THESE SITUATIONS SOUND FAMILIAR?

☐ You sense the senior pastor doesn't trust you. His message is subtle, but obvious, "We hired you to work with these kids, but you should do it the way *I* want it done." The double message painfully pricks at your self-esteem and sense of worth. How can you effectively be in ministry when you're not in control?

☐ You know what the kids at your church need, but Sue is the youth board chairwoman. And that's bad news. She has an insatiable need to control every meeting; she squelches ideas that aren't her own. You can predict her parting words, "What you really ought to do is . . ."

☐ None of the congregation's members seem to know what's going on with *those* kids, and So-and-so isn't satisfied with whatever does happen. Things are okay as long as the church kitchen is off-limits for the youth. Whenever the youth group and another church board have mistakenly scheduled two meetings for the same room, the youth group has to move its meeting.

☐It's been a year now and you still haven't figured out what the senior pastor expects of you. Most of the time you settle for trying to read her mind and guessing what you're supposed to do. She avoids conversations and seems conveniently busy when you want to talk.

If any or all of these strike a twinge of hurt within you, you're probably struggling with how to handle authority.

LEARNING TO BE NO. 2

It's inevitable. Working in the world of youth ministry means you're No. 2. You must answer to church boards, report to senior pastors and inform congregations. Survival implies learning to handle the "powers that be." It's crucial to remember that being involved in youth ministry means you're never alone. And that's good! It's being a part *of*, not apart *from*, the church. With that blessing of being connected comes the challenge of dealing with authority.

For starters, look to the One whose servant-style we strive to follow. From a human point of view, Jesus' way of life seems like nonsense. Who else goes around saying things such as "The first shall be last and the last shall be first?" Or how about that foolish way of life that demands that you die to yourself to be really alive? And then there's the whole list of people who will inherit the kingdom of God: the poor, the mourning, the humble, the persecuted. How's that for not making any sense? Jesus must have lived on another planet. "Though he was in the form of God, did not count equality with God a thing to be grasped, but emptied himself, taking the form of a servant, being born in the likeness of men" (Philippians 2:6-7). Isn't that crazy? Absurd?

Maybe. Maybe not.

God challenges us to live upside down, inside out and contrary to what comes naturally. The God of all creation freely emptied himself to be everyone's servant. The Greek word "doulos" means the lowliest form of servant, one enslaved, enthralled, subservient in ministry. More than once the word "doulos" describes Jesus and our response in faith. In this servant example we find truths for strengthening relationships. It's not easy. In fact, we fumble and fail as we attempt to grasp the total vision of being a servant.

BECOMING NO. 1 BY BEING NO. 2

An exciting opportunity awaits you as you learn to approach authority from this perspective. Read on and you will discover five steps for making servant-style your style.

Know your own worth. Isn't there a Bible passage somewhere that says love your church board and senior pastor as yourself? Whoever it is you're to love, the Bible makes it clear that it's the "you," not the "who," that matters. If you doubt your own value and worth as a person, you will never get beyond resentment, bitterness and anger in handling authority. Until your faith moves you to trust that you are a loved, worthwhile instrument of God, those in authority will threaten you. When you forget the need to prove yourself, you can move into loving and initiating positive interaction. Love yourself. You are a unique, valuable, special servant God is using to minister to young people, their parents and the pastor.

Keep communication open. Open, continued communication—servant-style—involves risk on your part. Don't wait for the senior pastor to come to you first. Don't expect the church board's built-in radar to detect that you're struggling. Reach out. Be a risk-taker, a first-move maker. That's frightening and humbling, but essential, in dealing with someone in authority. Communicating means taking the time to set up an appointment to discuss your feelings or attend that seemingly unnecessary board meeting.

Even if the person, board or congregation never asks you for information, keep them informed anyway. The wider the base of people who are aware of what you're doing in youth ministry, the more diminished the misunderstandings and suspicions.

Share your youth ministry dreams and nightmares. Express your joys and frustrations. Ephesians 4:15-16 holds a gem of truth: "By speaking the truth in a spirit of love, we must grow up in every way to Christ who is head. Under his control all the different parts of the body fit together by every joint with which it is provided. So when each separate part works as it should, the whole body grows and builds itself up through love."

Not only is it vital to communicate with those in authority, but also with special people you trust. Find a support system. Carefully choose one or two confidants with whom you

can tell your deeper struggles. Make certain they are
friends who keep conversations in confidence.

Be giving and forgiving. Just hearing the word "servant"
conjures up images of garbage collectors, gas station attend-
ants or waiters. They're those forgotten folks who do the
dirty work and get little, if any credit. From a Christlike
perspective, giving means stretching, extending and going
beyond yourself from feeling "I *have* to" to "I *want* to."

Giving means offering yourself without expecting reward
or credit. It doesn't mean giving in or giving up. A servant
isn't a doormat to be trod upon and trampled. A servant
isn't a loser or an expendable commodity. Giving involves
working with, not against, each other. Responsibility for
smooth relationships should flow from both sides. We forget
God has placed people in our lives as leaders. "Obey your
leaders and follow their orders. They watch over your souls
without resting, since they must give to God an account of
their service." Notice: The verse says *their* service! This
portion of Hebrews 13:17 adds a dimension of their giving
and service to you also.

Forgiving goes with giving. We accept people for whom
they are, letting go of the wrongs they've done. Separating
the person from the hurtful action creates a loving distinction. We thank God for that distinction as he assures us of
his care and forgiveness. Our Lord challenges us to "Go,
then, and do the same."

Walk a mile in their shoes. To handle authority more effectively, empathize with those in leadership positions. Get
into their shoes, their skin, their job descriptions. What does
it feel like to be the one labeled "in authority"? Imagine
these potential feelings:

Threatened: "Our youth ministry program has skyrocketed
since we put that new youth director in charge. All kinds of
exciting things are happening now."

Excluded: "All the kids are dropping by to talk to the
youth counselors. The kids never stop by to say hello to me."

Suspicious: "What do they do at those youth meetings anyway? Sounds like they have too much fun. They couldn't possibly be studying the Bible too!"

Guilty: "What do you mean, you don't know what's going
on with our church's youth? You're supposed to be on top of
things."

Relief: "Whew! It's about time we found someone to work with those kids. I'm exhausted and need a break."

God believes in empathy and understanding, so he became one of us. Our Servant One did just that! We trust in a God who cared enough to walk a mile (and more) in our shoes.

BE PATIENT

Being a servant is a lifelong process of personal growth. Relationships require tremendous energy, time and work. So watch for the little successes in handling authority. Delight in the times she didn't say, "I'm too busy to talk." Rejoice over the council meeting in which the pastor said the youth are making a difference in the congregation. Celebrate the times you held your temper and simply listened.

Patience and faith are partners. "For your life is a matter of faith, not of sight" (2 Corinthians 5:7). Even when you're unable to see results from your servant-style, trust God is at work. He won't abandon you. You are a treasured servant!

ADDITIONAL READING

The Multiple Staff and the Larger Church, Lyle E. Schaller, Abingdon.

CHAPTER

25

How to Get Along With Your Senior Pastor

BY J. DAVID STONE

Perhaps the reason for the average short job span of a youth worker (20 or so months in any one church) is his or her inability to get along with the senior pastor. It's sad, but I believe true.

I suspect that many youth workers become disillusioned the first year or so from trying to live down the previous youth director hero—proving himself or herself trustworthy with youth, parents and congregation, and trying desperately to please the senior pastor. It is no wonder that an invitation from another church (disguised as "the call") for a higher salary and more youth (disguised as a "bigger challenge") seems so attractive. Yet, job jumping as an answer to all frustration is seldom fulfilling—rarely does it help the youth worker feel like more than a failure. I know. I've been there.

What we really need is someone to stand with us through all the hassles, be there when we experience joy and especially support us when we sorrow. I am confident that your pastor is that person.

Developing that support isn't always easy. During the past 20 years I have worked with the "Do-it-according-to-the-book" pastor; the "Plodder"; the "Let's pray about it" pastor; the "Whing-ding, hang on, super extravaganza" spiritual leader; the "I'm always right, of course" preacher; and the "Look, but don't touch" pastor. I have been called on the carpet, under the carpet, in the carpet and had to pay for the carpet. I have been used, abused, praised, cut down, farmed out, talked about, honored, questioned as to my spiritual integrity, manipulated, lied to, loved, liked and "worried about." I've had my budget cut, shared a secretary, been criticized for being gone so much, fought with the choir director, sat through four-hour staff meetings, almost lost my family, missed meals, said the wrong things to the wrong person, forgot names, broke the projector, lost the keys, forgot communion and bombed out. About everything that could happen to a youth director has happened to me. It's a wonder I survived . . . more wonder that my youth groups did.

Although we are called to be faithful and not successful, whether the youth program will survive depends to a great extent on the youth worker's rapport with the senior pastor.

The following suggestions are not to be construed as "gimmicks" to deceive your pastor, but as solid human relation skills which will enable you to grow together in the faith instead of merely "getting along."

These ideas may sound a bit manipulative. They are. Manipulation is not all bad. But remember one cardinal rule: Anything you do should be done sincerely or there will be no power to what you do.

In fact, some of the best advice I can give you is to not "try so hard." When you overly exert yourself at anything, you feel unnatural, and the pastor will know you are not being genuine. Faking your actions or emotions will do you more harm than good in the long run.

Every youth director's situation with a senior pastor is different, of course, but the basic human relation skills are essentially the same.

RECOGNIZE THAT THE PASTOR IS "BOSS"

The pastor has the last word. Period. The pastor may be willing to share the big decision-making responsibilities with the staff, but the "buck" stops with him or her. Acknowledge that relationship by calling the pastor "Boss" or "Chief" occasionally. It's a subtle and joking way to let him or her know that you recognize where the power really is.

I remember going to see my pastor just after I had been hired as a youth director in a large church with a huge staff. I walked into his office, addressed him by name and announced that I was glad to serve as youth director in his ministry. I affirmed to him that his task was immense as the congregation's spiritual director and coordinator. I also told him that I wanted our relationship to be open and would appreciate all suggestions at any time.

I stated further that I would be loyal to his leadership unless it compromised my own Christian faith. "If that ever happens, I will come to you first," I said. "I will not talk to anyone else about the conflict before I come to you. You can count on it."

That brief encounter with my pastor cleared the air about a number of things up front and was the preamble of an excellent working relationship.

INVOLVE THE PASTOR IN THE YOUTH PROGRAM

One of the most embarrassing experiences for a pastor is not knowing a young person's name and why he or she is waiting in the office. The pastor also feels threatened and tends to see the youth not as someone who is busily preparing for the senior drama group presentation, but as a kid who is dressed inappropriately and dripping paint everywhere.

Here is how to communicate about the events in your youth department:

● Make sure that the pastor gets a copy of the youth bulletin.

● Ask the pastor to announce from the pulpit on a regular basis the youth department's upcoming projects. It can be upsetting to a pastor to have to announce: "The youth group will be having a surprise program tonight" (which usually means, "The youth director doesn't have anything in mind yet").

● Following a young person's profession of faith, ask the pastor to contact the youth and discuss his or her decision. You will be delightfully surprised at the depth it will add to your program and the meaning it will have for the entire church community.

● In your program planning, include the pastor in some way at least once every two months. Believe it or not, pastors can do more than preach and show Holy Land slides. Plan an "Ask the Pastor Night" or sing a duet with the pastor in front of the total group or build a program around the morning sermon and invite the pastor to answer questions. Let the pastor install youth group officers. Ask the pastor to serve communion at the close of a retreat or lead the prayer just before boarding the bus to leave on a trip.

● Sending memos is not a bad idea if you don't wear out the idea. Send a memo in your own handwriting (if it's typed, he'll wonder if that is all you have to do) to remind him of special events or when a young person has done something noteworthy in school or the community.

● Attempt to schedule staff meetings each week with the pastor. Or perhaps you could manage a weekly session to update the pastor. Keep those update sessions under 15 minutes; otherwise, there may not be anymore update sessions.

● The size of the church often will dictate the pastor's availability. You will probably have to compete for his time, but don't hesitate to do that. The larger the church, the more exposure he or she needs to the youth group!

BE A PASTOR TO THE PASTOR

I know, you say, "He won't let me minister to him" or, "Our age difference keeps me from being a pastor to the pastor." Where do you think the pastor turns for support or a spiritual uplift? The places are unfortunately unlimited, and it seems everybody thinks the pastor is a spiritual giant who doesn't need any "propping up."

● Note the times when the pastor seems depressed. Don't ask him about the problem if you don't have a close relationship. Instead, be thoughtful: put fruit on his desk with a brief note of appreciation or have the youth group carol him even though it's not Christmas. (Note: This must be genuine or it will be awkward.) Give him some good news. Suggest that you will set up or clean up the meeting room since you're going to be around that area anyway. Don't do anything that says, "Hey, look at me; I'm taking care of you!"

● Pray for your pastor. Organize the youth to meet each Sunday before the worship service to pray for the service and guidance for the pastor. It won't be long before your pastor will feel that powerful support.

● Drop hints that you support the pastor. Before an important meeting the pastor is going to lead, whisper to him, "Hey, I'm thinking about you," or "I'm with you." You'll be surprised how much that helps not only the pastor, but you too.

● Give the pastor credit for good ideas. Not just to his or her face, but in public. I have never sincerely bragged on someone without receiving a blessing. You will not only endear yourself to the pastor by affirming that he or she is not dumb in your eyes, but your acknowledgment will give him or her more credibility with the youth group.

COMMON SENIOR PASTOR QUESTIONS

In my travels across the country and in my workshops, several questions frequently are asked about getting along with senior pastors. The following questions are the most common:

Q: I need help and guidance in my part of the ministry, but everyone else is too busy doing his or her own things. What should I do?

A: I have discovered that those who are doing "their own thing" are usually just as frustrated as I am, but they cover it up by keeping busy. "When you're busy, you don't have time to think about it" is the excuse. If you are in a situation such as this, the best thing I have found to do is:

● Ask for help, have a proposed plan in writing. Show your plan to your superior or co-worker and ask how best to improve it. Otherwise, your co-worker may think your request for help is only a subconscious method of getting attention. One of our problems in intra-staff communication is that we simply don't ask for what we want. If you don't ask, you surely won't get what you want.

● Ask for a regular time to get together as a staff to check signals and talk about the big picture—the overall ministry of the church.

Do not be surprised at the amount of support you receive when you ask for help or state your feelings about everyone else being too busy doing his or her own thing. Everyone is probably feeling the same way. You might even be a hero for mentioning it. At any rate, to ask for guidance does not mean you are second-rate. It indicates how smart you are!

Q: Deep inside I feel that there's a problem, but I don't know what it is.

A: I don't know either. No one else does. There is, however, a data bank inside each of us that stores all knowledge about us. If you can program it properly, not only will you discover the problem, but more than likely find a solution. Here is the formula:

● Ask yourself, *"What do I want?"* (If you ask yourself that question, you must answer if it's going to do any good.)

● Follow that question with, *"What am I feeling?"* What is the emotion? Identify that emotion. The closer you get in touch with your emotion, the closer you are to the real you.

● The third question to ask is, *"What am I doing to get what I want?"* You may discover that you are really not doing anything or at the most, not much.

● After asking those questions one time, ask them again, this time requiring different answers. Repeat the process several times. Then ask, *"What do I need to do?"*

Follow that question to conclusion: *"Will I do it? When? How?"*

Q: I'm afraid of my pastor. What should I do?

A: Have you ever worried about something for a long period of time only to discover that the outcome was not as bad as you had feared? Many professionals will tell you that your mind does tricks, and that given a small amount of information and a few coincidences, almost any idea can be blown out of proportion. I know that is true. I've experienced it.

I remember my pastor suggesting that I visit a particular family because they were having trouble with their teenage son. I had every intention to visit the family, but each time I planned to go something else came up.

My pastor would ask every now and then if I had made

that visit. Of course, I explained that I was planning to, but had not gotten around to it. I don't know why I didn't make that visit a priority. I never made the visit.

Eventually, the teenager ran away from home. I blamed myself. I just knew the pastor and everybody else blamed me too. I dodged my pastor for days, afraid of him. Surely he was disappointed in me and given the right opportunity would expose my negligence or fire me.

That small incident began to take on larger and larger proportions. I felt more inadequate as a youth director and as though I had let everybody down, especially my pastor. My job began to show it. I kept to myself more because I was afraid of a confrontation. Finally, at my wit's end, I walked into my pastor's office and blurted out my story. I must say I was scared!

That visit turned out to be one of the best actions I've ever made. After discussing my fear, I discovered my pastor never harbored any ill will for me and was relieved that the real reason for my ignoring him was because of my fear of what he thought. I learned from that experience:

● Probably any fear that I have of my pastor is contrived and is easily dissipated by communicating.

● I needed to know my pastor better, and sharing my shortcomings with him and asking for his guidance and support not only complimented him (my pastor has wisdom), but made me a better youth director.

● When I have a problem with anyone, I handle it immediately. The longer I wait, the worse it gets.

● As I take ownership of my faith and work at maintaining integrity in my work, then that's all I am required to do. God does the rest. I am simply called to be faithful!

Getting along with your senior pastor is not a game of guessing what he or she wants from you. Nor is it a "buttering up" contest. The best way to get along with your senior pastor is to use common sense and follow your best intuitive plan. Probably the biggest barrier to having a good, healthy, productive relationship hinges on your good, healthy, productive attitude. Remember that your pastor is just as human as you are and has needs just as you do. Your task is simply to realize that both of you are in the ministry to validate the love of Christ in each other and to each other.

ADDITIONAL READING

The Multiple Staff and the Larger Church, Lyle E. Schaller, Abingdon.

Survival Tactics in the Parish, Lyle E. Schaller, Abingdon.

Section 3

MANAGING YOUR FAMILY LIFE

One key to a successful ministry is keeping a perspective on your priorities. Evaluate and refine the delicate balance between your ministry and the rest of your life.

How to Keep Your Life and Ministry Balanced

BY JOHN SHAW

A friend of yours works seven days a week and he rarely takes vacations. Which of those comments might you make?
a. You're wonderful! I've never seen such commitment.
b. No comment. It's his business how much he works.
c. You're doing a lot of good work, but you'll burn yourself out at the rate you're going. Have you considered taking some time off?

Your spouse/best friend complains that you "never" take your day(s) off. How might you reply?
a. Never say "never."
b. I can't help it. My ministry demands a lot of time.
c. You're right. I'll clear my days off so we can have some time together.

One of the parents of a kid in your youth group is pushing for a three-week summer bike tour for the youth group. This new program would fill every week of the summer

**with church activities. Which one of these statements is
most like a response you'd make:**
  a. I'm not convinced of the effectiveness of bike touring as
     a Christian activity.
  b. That's a great idea. We'll make it happen somehow.
  c. My schedule is too full for me to become involved in
     another activity this summer. Will you take responsibil-
     ity for planning and sponsorship of the bike tour?

If you chose response "c" in each case, you may be working effectively toward a balanced Christian life. If you answered with the other responses, you may be heading toward an unbalanced lifestyle.

Keeping your lifestyle balanced is the key to an effective
lifelong ministry. You'll be able to accomplish significant
things if you can keep yourself refreshed and revitalized.

YOUR PRIORITIES

It takes careful planning and constant effort to keep every
important part of life alive and growing.

A total commitment to Christ makes it easy to assume that
ministry always takes precedence over everything else. But
getting totally caught up in church activities is a trap that
defeats the purpose of ministry itself.

Jesus placed a great emphasis on keeping the various
parts of life in proper perspective. He reprimanded Martha
who demanded that her sister "serve" him instead of wanting to just be with him.

Even serving Jesus must be suspended at times in order to
build a relationship with him. The same principle holds true
for our other responsibilities. Family, friends and self all are
important. They demand time and energy as part of our
stewardship of life.

YOUR PERSONAL NEEDS

Caring for ourselves also takes a conscious effort. Jesus
pointed out to Martha that Mary's personal needs took precedence over "serving." We need to remember not only to
develop a personal relationship with Christ, but also to provide for personal needs.

Hebrews 4:10-11 points out that we're not better than
God, who took a day of rest after a week's labor. To do less
than take one day of rest each week is being disobedient.

God has a reason for demanding that we take regular weekly rest. We can become entangled in our work and lose sight of our purpose for existing. It's good for us to realize that our work with young people is a small, though vital, part of God's broad purpose for our lives.

Perhaps the most pitiable person is the youth minister who becomes driven by his or her own program. The youth complain that he or she doesn't have enough time for them. When this situation occurs, family and friends usually complain too. The youth program has become an obsession. Priorities are dangerously imbalanced.

Jesus knew the importance of keeping a clear picture of what he was trying to accomplish. Often, he would draw apart from the pressing responsibilities of his ministry to meditate and pray. Immediately after his baptism and in preparation for his ministry, Jesus identified his priorities. The temptations in the wilderness helped him clarify his commitment to God before starting an everyday ministry among people (Matthew 4:1-11).

Getting swallowed up by our work habits often causes us to lose sight of God's creative effort to fill our lives with newness. A well-placed timeout for rest and personal development can break through those stubborn habits and keep us open to God's refreshing actions.

YOUR NEED FOR BALANCE

One way to keep life in balance is to know when life is getting off keel. A healthy self-consciousness helps. We also need sensitive awareness of how other people feel or react to us.

Self-consciousness helps us identify symptoms of an unbalanced life. Internal signals need our attention. We can become aware of these signals by asking certain questions:

- Can I relax?
- Is it easy to get to sleep at night?
- Do I wake up in the morning feeling refreshed?
- Is it hard to maintain concentration?
- Do I have physical aches and pains for no apparent reason?
- Do I feel apathetic and listless, or do I have energy and vitality?
- What is my attitude toward unexpected changes in

plans, new information, challenges? (Do I dread changes or do I tackle new challenges with confidence?)

Interpersonal signals furnish clues to the balances in our lives:

● What attitude do I receive from my spouse? children? friends?

● Do they have their own patterns of life that largely ignore me? (If I'm not around much, how can they involve me in their lifestyles?)

External signals also reveal problems with life balancing:

● Do I pay my bills regularly? (Or, am I late and sometimes forget to pay?)

● Do my living quarters look like a disaster area?

● Are my shoes polished?

● Are my clothes clean and pressed?

● Is my car kept up?

If we discover problems in some of these areas, we can begin immediately to make some changes. The first big step is to decide to change.

Pick one item from the list of unbalanced areas. Start with an item that could be changed fairly quickly such as paying bills or learning relaxation techniques. Set a reasonable goal for correcting the problem: *"I will learn relaxation techniques within the next two weeks"* or *"I will pay my bills by Friday night."*

For other items on the problem list, develop a plan for change. Brainstorm possibilities for new weekly work patterns that allow time for family and personal enrichment. Schedule a dramatic surprise for your spouse such as spending a full day alone together. Set up a special outing; plan a visit with some mutually enjoyable friends. Do whatever you can to make a memorable impact.

Set up a plan for spending more quality time on a regular basis with persons who mean the most to you. Work at sharing yourself with them and listening to what they have to share. (Don't be surprised if the first sharings carry some anger about past absences.) Give your full attention to these important people. Plan for situations and locations in which there will be no distractions from this sharing process.

Work out a time each day for meditation, scripture reading and prayer. Pick a place and time that prevents interruptions. Early morning is good for this kind of personal time, since little scheduling takes place then.

Use personal time to monitor and evaluate your balancing of the various areas of life. Give yourself a check-up once a week to see if any continuing problems need attention. (Look

---

ARE YOUR LIFE AND MINISTRY IN BALANCE?

Rank yourself from 1 to 5 in each of the following areas (1 is great and 5 is terrible):

1. I can relax.	1	2	3	4	5
2. It's easy for me to get to sleep at night.	1	2	3	4	5
3. I wake up in the morning feeling refreshed.	1	2	3	4	5
4. I can concentrate.	1	2	3	4	5
5. I can explain my aches and pains.	1	2	3	4	5
6. I feel impassive and listless.	1	2	3	4	5
7. I am an example of energy and vitality.	1	2	3	4	5
8. I can handle unexpected changes or challenges.	1	2	3	4	5
9. My family and friends have a great attitude about my life's balance.	1	2	3	4	5
10. I pay my bills regularly.	1	2	3	4	5
11. My house or apartment is usually fairly neat and clean.	1	2	3	4	5
12. I keep myself looking neat and clean.	1	2	3	4	5
13. I keep my car maintained.	1	2	3	4	5
14. I have a plan for keeping my life balanced.	1	2	3	4	5
15. I am included in the "patterns" of my family and friends.	1	2	3	4	5

Evaluate your responses and circle the three areas that need the most work. Then apply the steps listed in this article directly to your life.

for the "signals" mentioned earlier.)

When life begins to get back into balance, you'll begin to feel a oneness with God. You'll feel mutual understanding with family and friends. Life will seem to flow more smoothly. You'll begin to feel at home inside yourself. You'll believe that your current efforts and goals have value, meaning and purpose. And they will.

ADDITIONAL READING

Christian Renewal: Living Beyond Burnout, Charles L. Rassieur, Westminster.

Pastoral Care of Families, by William E. Hulme, Abingdon.

Stress/Unstress, Keith W. Sehnert, Augsburg.

Marriage to a youth pastor
is a rollercoaster ride—fun,
exciting and unpredictable
with great ups and downs.

CHAPTER
27

I Married a Youth Minister

BY MARY LOU CONWAY

Exciting, fast-paced, unpredictable. How can I describe being married to a youth minister? It's a circus, a bus station and a hospital emergency room all rolled into one big bundle.

If there were schools to prepare people to be married to youth ministers, the courses would range from "Counseling 101" to "Packing-Seven-Kids-Into-a-Back-Seat" and "500-Uses-for-Six-Dozen-Leftover-Hot-Dog-Buns." The traits most needed by such a person are ingenuity, luck, stubbornness and lots of love.

When we were first married, I tried to follow Bob everywhere. It was really a madhouse, balancing my full-time job with trying to keep up with my spouse in the evenings and on weekends. I learned a valuable lesson, one I try never to forget. I am not the youth pastor. I don't have to be my spouse's clone. I've learned that I don't need to solve the youth group's problems by myself.

My hardest adjustment has been the frequent separations from my spouse. I work days and my youth minister husband attends many evening meetings and weekend retreats. I have a few suggestions for dealing with this situation if you feel loneliness during those times:

● Prayer and Bible study are my greatest assets. I've worked through many Bible studies on weekends when I'm feeling the loneliest. Sometimes it seems that my prayer life is much stronger when I'm spending a weekend alone.

● Hobbies are wonderful to fill the time. I enjoy needle-point.

● I also correspond with many friends across the country. It's a good opportunity to keep in touch with everyone.

● A close friend within walking distance of home is a wonderful help. Sometimes you just need to talk with someone.

NOTES FROM A YOUTH MINISTER'S SPOUSE

Midnight telephone calls and emergency situations were difficult for me at first. Before getting married I had had little contact with the police, little experience with life-and-death situations at hospitals and little exposure to those on drugs.

I tend to cry during pressured interpersonal situations. But I've learned that my sensitivity and compassion are an asset in being there for kids who have a problem.

Drugs are a problem no matter what neighborhood, social class or income bracket. It helps to gain a knowledge of drugs, drug slang and to recognize a "high" youth.

Puppy love is a common ailment among teenage girls, as are fantasy-producing crushes among teenage guys. It is not uncommon for the youth minister to be the object of that infatuation. Talk out your feelings and the situation with your spouse. Let your spouse know that you trust him or her. When it comes to dealing with puppy love, the youth pastor needs an objective third party, in addition to his or her spouse. That third party can help sort out situations and offer an objective perspective on these interpersonal relationships. Remember, most kids quickly turn their attentions to people their own age.

Include young people in your life, as much as you feel comfortable. Being pregnant added a new dimension to my family's church life. Every youth in our group had an opinion on whether the baby would be a boy or a girl and when he or she would be born. When John was born, several youth stayed in the hospital waiting room and were allowed to see him when he was just minutes old. When John was baptized, we chose two youth as godparents.

A youth pastor's child is "adopted" as the youth group's young brother or sister and is welcomed as a part of the extended family. John isn't an only child; he has 150 brothers and sisters.

Yet, no matter how many youth group brothers and sisters a youth pastor's child has, I've learned that John needs his own private family—a time for our own special family life.

Time is a precious commodity. We set family and personal events in advance and fight to keep from changing them. Our goal as a family is to spend quality time together. It's also important for our son to spend time just being alone with his father.

Youth ministry is important. So is our family. So is my relationship with my spouse. Sometimes I have to change my plans. Sometimes my husband has to change his plans. Sometimes we compromise.

As a family we've learned to talk about our priorities and to keep our personal, family, spiritual and ministry priorities in a sensitive balance.

ADDITIONAL READING

Achieving the Impossible: Intimate Marriage, Charles M. Sell, Multnomah.

I Need to Have You Know Me, Roland and Doris Larson, Winston-Seabury.

Your Pastor's Problems, William E. Hulme, Abingdon.

Are you there for everyone
except your family? Per-
haps you need to arrange
your day so that you have
special family times.

CHAPTER
28

Where Does Your Family Rate in Your Life?

BY LARRY KEEFAUVER

Take this youth-worker-and-family quiz.

1. I dread the weekends, knowing that much of my free time will be involved with the youth.

   a. Never b. Seldom c. Occasionally d. Often e. Always

2. Sundays seem like an endless marathon. Come Monday, I'm exhausted.

   a. Never b. Seldom c. Occasionally d. Often e. Always

3. I feel guilty when I leave the house to go to a youth event. I feel as though I'm neglecting my family.

   a. Never b. Seldom c. Occasionally d. Often e. Always

4. My family shows signs of resenting the time I spend with the youth.

   a. Never b. Seldom c. Occasionally d. Often e. Always

5. I am reluctant to plan youth events the young people express need for knowing how much preparation and time will be needed.

   a. Never   b. Seldom   c. Occasionally   d. Often   e. Always

Do you find yourself experiencing some of these feelings? I've been there. Years ago in my first youth ministry position, every night of the week was filled with "church." Most weekends were jammed with lock-ins, car washes, retreats, clowning, school functions and church services.

On one typical Sunday, with the day packed full of activities from Sunday school through evening youth fellowships, I met my family in the church parking lot. I kissed my wife hello and goodbye for the day and gave the children hugs.

She asked, "Will you be home this afternoon?"

"No, dear," I replied, "there's not enough time between bell choir, youth choir, youth council meeting and snack supper. See you this evening."

"Don't bother," she replied, "I won't be there when you get home."

It wasn't hard for me to guess that something was wrong. As she drove off without a look or kiss, I knew it! I canceled that day's workload and proceeded home for some serious face-to-face discussion.

That warning helped turn my life around. I know that Jesus Christ is the center and power of my life. I also know that the most important human support system I have is my family. When positive, intimate relationships happen at home, I can work and cope well. When the home scene is in turmoil, nothing goes right!

Here are some pointers to help you remember and minister to those sometimes forgotten people at home:

SCHEDULE TIME FOR YOUR FAMILY

Set aside at least two, and if possible, three uninterrupted evenings at home with your family, focusing on their needs. If necessary take the phone off the hook or get an answering machine. Spending time at home doing paperwork or talking "church" or "youth" matters on the phone is not spending time with the family. Get up earlier if you need to spend more time with youth ministry planning.

Remember, time spent with your family when you're hungry or fatigued diminishes its significance. Work at spending intentional one-to-one, face-to-face time with each family member.

PRAY DAILY FOR FAMILY MEMBERS.

I heard Lloyd John Ogilvie reflect in a session, "Intercessory prayer is not as much us placing our burdens on God, as God placing his burdens on us." When we pray for our family members individually and for their specific needs, we become open to how God may use us to touch those needs.

MAKE DATES WITH YOUR FAMILY

Beyond the daily, face-to-face encounters, set significant blocks of time (three to four hours) for at least monthly, one-to-one dates with spouse and children. This is a special time for doing what they enjoy with you, away from church and normal family routine. Plan in advance and clear your schedule. Keep your promises. Cancel only for emergencies and then reschedule the date as soon as possible.

GIVE YOUR FULL ATTENTION

Whenever you're with family, give your full self. Often we are present physically with a family member, but our thoughts and feelings are wrapped up in work. Be present in body and spirit. Listening attentively communicates worth and warmth.

Our families are God's gift to us. We need to reverence, cherish, and edify our families.

What does it mean if I touch hundreds of people in the church,
    And my family is untouched?
What is it worth if I lead countless youth to Christ,
    And my children are lost?
What if masses enjoy hearing me speak,
    And my family never hears from me?
What is gained if I'm present and here for others who suffer,
    While my family members are lonely and hurting?

Take time to pray about your family priorities. Be there for your family.

Unmarried ministers need others—they cannot go it alone. They need to build supportive relationships both in and out of the church.

Unmarried Youth Leaders And 'Family' Support

BY LARRY KEEFAUVER

A lot has been written about the special needs of married pastors and their families, but little has been addressed to those ministers who are single. Married ministers generally can turn to their families for support, but where does the single pastor turn?

The people from whom they draw their support are somewhat different, but the following needs are critical and remain basically the same: affirmation, encouragement and prayer from nurturing individuals.

Single youth ministers as well as other single adults can no longer be viewed as a small minority of the population. The U.S. Census Bureau reports that about 40 percent of the adult population is single and says that figure will climb to 50 percent before this decade ends. The Census Bureau predicts that by the end of the 1980s, there will be more single than married adults in the United States. The needs of the single ministers are important now and will become more important as their numbers increase.

Although it may seem less troublesome to be single, the

fact remains: Singles need others to help support them— they cannot go it alone. They need someone to share with in times of rejoicing, someone to help them in times of trouble.

Married ministers generally have a built-in support system—their families. Single youth ministers have to build their own support systems from family, friends and colleagues.

How can a single youth minister improve his or her support system? One helpful exercise is to make a list of five nurturing persons in his or her life. These would be people a youth minister could go to for a relaxing time of friendship, sharing, prayer, support and affirmation. Some of these people may be:

● family members such as parents, brothers, sisters, aunts or uncles.

● friends or support groups within the church.

● youth ministry professionals in the community or within the leader's own denomination.

● Christians outside the local church such as friends from high school or college days.

Once a youth minister has made a list of five nurturing persons, he or she should try to increase the list to 10. Some of these nurturing persons need to live close geographically. Others may live hundreds of miles away, but through correspondence, telephone calls, and occasional face-to-face encounters at retreats and seminars, the youth minister can keep close contact.

If you, as a single youth minister, do not have at least five to 10 nurturing persons, you may not have the sense of a "family" support system needed for youth ministry.

Church leaders and staff may well be a family within the church for a single youth minister, but they're not the only family source needed. The minister also needs nurturing structures such as Bible study groups, prayer cells or Sunday school classes. If a single youth minister consciously and intentionally reaches out for nurturing family support, he or she will enhance and build the strength of ministry.

It is also important to realize that other Christians in our support system need us. Sometimes because a single youth minister's time is abused and misused by the church, there isn't enough time left for others. Churches often believe that a single youth minister has more free time than a married

youth minister, and therefore can work more hours. This is
an illusion. The single youth minister needs to be in a family
support relationship with other brothers and sisters in
Christ, inside and outside the church, not just a working relationship with them.

I often have heard friends of single youth ministers complain that they never see them, rarely receive telephone
calls, and often have no opportunity to pray or enjoy a social
time with them. This is tragic. The single youth minister
needs family support outside of his or her immediate ministry area and they need him or her.

It becomes important, then, to have at least one or two
days off a week and two to three evenings a week free. The
single youth minister must schedule free time because it simply will not come naturally. In scheduling free time, the
single youth minister needs to plan activities of self-mainte-
nance such as prayer, Bible study, recreation, exercise and
quiet time. These personal maintenance, "being-good-to-
myself" activities, are critical for sustaining ministry to
youth.

Jesus' great commandment focuses on loving God with all
of one's being, loving neighbor and loving oneself. The single
youth ministry professional has no more time to love self,
others and God than anyone else. Since that is the case, it is
important to schedule and prioritize times so that personal
growth, family-style relationships with others, as well as
serving God in ministry, are maintained daily. When a youth
minister actively seeks to build a nurturing support family
outside of his or her professional ministry, then the reality
becomes realized that one is a whole number and not a
lonely number.

There are two models for single ministry in the New Tes-
tament—Jesus and Paul. They took time apart from the
crowd and the ministry for themselves and for God. They
also had personal friends. Paul sent greetings to lists of extended families all over the Mediterranean world. Jesus had
not only his close disciples as a family support group, he
also had personal friends throughout Galilee and Judea. The
best-known of these were Martha, Mary and Lazarus. Jesus
and Paul demonstrated that ministry as a single is possible
in its fullness and wholeness to the glory of God. As singles,
we must go for a ministry that includes a wholeness of

family nurturing that builds us up and enables us to minister in the name of Jesus Christ.

ADDITIONAL READING

Celebrating the Single Life: A Spirituality for Single Persons in Today's World, Susan Annette Muto, Doubleday.

The Friendship Factor, Alan Loy McGinnis, Augsburg.

Saturday Night, Sunday Morning: Singles and the Church, Nicholas B. Christoff, Harper and Row.

Section 4
MANAGING YOUR SELF

Is your 24-hour-a-day job out of control? Rearranging your life and priorities can bring you renewed joy and enthusiasm.

CHAPTER 30

Does Your Ministry Control You?

BY JAMES C. KOLAR

"**D**addy, look at me when I'm talking to you!" So demanded my daughter, who was 4 years old at the time, as she not-too-gently removed the newspaper from in front of my face.

I had come home from "one of those days" and quickly positioned myself on the couch with the newspaper in the serious attempt to avoid human contact for at least 20 minutes.

My daughter, however, had other ideas about how I should spend my time. I had barely finished the comics when she sat down next to me and began a preschooler's version of 100 questions. Having turned off my skills involving active listening, accurate empathy and unconditional positive regard, I answered her questions with grunts. And with a 4-year-old's perceptive insight into the dynamics of human interaction, she decided we needed eye contact to further pursue our discussion.

With her diagnosis intact, she took action. Although I never made it to the sports section, I did have more of a two-sided discussion with my daughter—and I had something to think about later that evening.

SERIOUS THINKING

What I thought about, or perhaps it would be more accurate to say *wondered* about, was why I had pursued so intently the goal of reading the newspaper. Spiderman, it's true, had been in a tight spot the day before, and Kerry Drake was in the midst of a midlife crisis. But even I could see that there had been more involved in my action than keeping up with the high drama of the comic-strip heroes.

I realized that I was more concerned with avoiding human contact than I had been interested in reading the paper. Because I had been with people all day and had more meetings scheduled that night, I just wanted to get away from it all for a while.

I realized I needed time away from the demands of work—demands which had to do with other people and what they needed, wanted, etc. When I had gotten that far in my wondering, three points came into focus.

The first was that I didn't relax very well or very much. Much of what I did under the name of relaxation was really escape—such as burying myself in the newspaper. The escape was occasioned by the need to divert myself from the pressures of unfinished work.

The second point that came into focus was that my work will never be finished. I can never meet all the needs and wants of the people I work with, whether they be youth, adults, other members of the staff or parents. I can work 24 hours a day, seven days a week, and I still won't be able to do everything that needs to be done.

There always will be people who need to talk, to learn, to be trained or encouraged. Knowing that, I thought I had adjusted my attitudes and expectations to conform to the reality of the situation. And yet, why did I always feel behind? I would fret that if I would work this next weekend or work later for the next few nights, times when I had planned to be off, maybe I could get caught up—or at least feel caught up.

As I thought about my past 12 years in ministry, I realized I'd never gotten to a point where my work was caught up and completed. One thing was never done before other things were coming up. It seemed that whenever I was at the end of one thing, I was in the middle of two others and at the beginning of several more.

There would always be planning, evaluations and programming. And then there were all the relational and personal situations, most of which were always in the stage called "the midst of things."

I discovered that my psychological and emotional life was geared to things being done, taken care of, in order, and all fixed up. I could only *really* relax when things were tidy and in good shape.

The third point I discovered was that I was taking myself too seriously. Deep down within me I found this mysterious little conviction that if God were going to get on in the world, he needed me to do it. If all these people were to be loved, listened to, forgiven, taught, trained, encouraged and converted, guess who God's invaluable little helper was going to be? Yup—you guessed it—me.

That incident with my daughter took place more than two years ago. And I learned I needed to change some of my attitudes and behavior. I have discovered some ways that work for me; let me share them with you.

HOW TO ENERGIZE AND ENJOY LIFE

"Enjoy the special days as they come." The first time I heard that German proverb I thought it was so obvious that it didn't need to be said. But its meaning was one I needed to grasp with more than my head.

With my tendency to want everything done and in order before I relax, I found myself in a similar position to the college student who goes home for the Thanksgiving holiday knowing that finals start the first week of December. The holiday is occupied with either studying for the finals or thinking and worrying about studying for the finals.

In ministry it's not the "finals," it's an activity or program that's coming up, or a talk that isn't finished or an unsolved relational problem. There's always something that's hanging over me. So I can either worry about it or I can enjoy the special days as they come.

Have an attitude of thankfulness. Put somewhat differently: When I am not thankful, I am not joyful.

Thankfulness is a major means of getting in touch with the good things that are happening in my life and in the world. It's a way of getting out of my self-contained and self-enclosed world that's filled with my plans, goals and efforts into the much bigger world of God's presence.

The simple starting point is the question, "What am I thankful for during these last three hours, this last day or last week?" I am not talking about all those big things we "should" be grateful for but rather the little, surprising things that happen in our day. These are the things that we wouldn't even remember unless we think about them: like the smile the salesperson had as I bought the birthday gift for my sister; or the letter from a former youth group member who just wanted to say "Hi"; or the song on the radio with the catchy, happy tune; or the time of sharing with a friend at breakfast.

Make time for things you want to do. For 10 years I had wanted to travel to northern Minnesota during the fall to go hiking. For nine years something important came up so that I couldn't go. This last year I put it on my schedule, and despite the important things, I went anyway. It was marvelous.

Taking time for things that I enjoy is a source of energy for me. I love to listen to classical music, as well as Irish and Scottish folk music. I try to take 15 or 20 minutes during a day to do that; I find myself more relaxed and at ease and more able to enjoy the rest of the day.

Pay attention to daydreams. At times those dreams have to do not only with what we enjoy but also with what we need. Oftentimes when we have been camping, after a few days of diet that's been composed mainly of freeze-dried and other unsubstantial food, the conversation will turn into a food fantasy of everybody's favorite dishes. In a similar way, a person who is thirsty often will daydream about something to drink.

When my mind wanders off in a certain direction, I ask myself if there is something more involved in that daydreaming. When's the last time I got away for more than a few hours? Do things that I'm doing take longer than they should? At times our daydreams have a great deal to say about not only what we enjoy but also what we need.

Change some of your activities. Doing something that is much different than we normally do can be a way to tap into a renewed source of vitality for our lives.

When so much of our work has to do with people who are

in need, in one way or another, we find we are giving part of ourselves to them. This has been compared to a "small but constant loss of blood." We give part of our energy to people in need; the result is often a depletion of our personal resources.

A way to renew our energy is to do something that can give life to us. Hiking, music, photography and simple physical labor are the things that I find great enjoyment in—and they are also things that give me energy.

I have found it important to distinguish, however, when those things become more escape than life-giving. The key for me is compulsion. When I have to do one or the other or when I have to get so much done, there's little enjoyment. When I can go into the activity with no overriding goals or objectives, I find it to be both enjoyable and energizing.

Spend time with people you enjoy. If you have never done it, you may want to make a list of people whom you enjoy being with and who give life to you. Do you make any effort to be with these people, or are your times with them dependent on circumstance? If the latter is true, consider being more intentional in getting together with them.

Set up a time in advance, just as you do with other things that are important. It may seem a bit too organized and unspontaneous, but it will allow you more time to be with those whom you enjoy. In the long run, you will have more strength and energy for your own life.

Plan your life so that you can hang in there for the long run. Finding those things and people that bring energy and joy into your life is a major way to stay in touch with the One who is the source of every good gift.

ADDITIONAL READING

Dare to Discipline Yourself, Dale E. Galloway, Revell.

Overcoming Indecisiveness, Theodore Rubin, Harper and Row.

The Work Trap, Ted W. Engstrom and David J. Juroe, Revell.

The demanding ministry to
youth isn't for everybody.
Do you have gifts to make
it a long-term calling?

CHAPTER

31

Youth Work: Stepping Stone or Lifelong Career?

BY RICH BIMLER

"**I**'ve about had it with being a youth worker. I'm just kind of burned out."

"Give me five good years as a youth minister, and I'll be ready to move on to something else."

"What are you going to do when you get older and won't be able to work with the youth?"

Perhaps you have heard, or even murmured, some of those statements. Such thoughts continually surface among people who work with youth. To some, youth ministry is a stepping stone to a "more significant" ministry. To others, youth ministry is for the "young ministers," those still able and interested in playing basketball or slumbering in sleeping bags at a retreat.

I still can remember my intense feelings one Friday night, many years ago, during a lock-in in the church basement. Three congregations were represented, with more than 75 young people swarming practically out of control. The two other youth ministers and I became frustrated and annoyed as the evening went on. I remember the three of us, all mature adults, looking at one another and saying: "How did we get ourselves into this? Isn't there an easier way to make a living?"

LENGTH OF COMMITMENT

Let's say loudly and clearly what needs to be said: Youth ministry is not only for the rookie minister or youngest person with the most energy. Youth ministry is for adults of every age. And youth ministry should be seen as a full-time, lifelong position.

Youth ministry is nothing less than crucial. The youth years are probably the most difficult years for teaching, understanding, communicating. The junior and senior high years are intense periods of questioning values of the adult world, exercising newly acquired intellectual capabilities and preparing for breaking away from the family. Loving, dedicated and spiritually sensitive leaders can be the catalysts for lifelong decisions.

But for some youth workers, volunteers and professionals, youth ministry isn't necessarily a forever commitment.

What's the difference? It's simply in the type of gifts God has given you. For those adults blessed with certain abilities and talents, youth ministry can be a satisfying lifetime ministry profession. But for those ministers involved in youth ministry who find out, either suddenly or gradually, that their gifts are better suited for a different type of ministry, great! Let them move into that ministry without feelings of guilt or failure.

A PERILOUS STEPPING STONE

Starting on the bottom rung, as many youth leaders see it, and moving from church to church, youth group to youth group in an attempt to move higher on the ministry ladder can be dangerous.

Youth ministry is built on relationships among people. Relationships are built on trust. It doesn't take many upwardly mobile youth leaders who say "Trust me" but leave after less than two years, to add support to the ever-strengthening barriers that youth erect to protect themselves from being hurt.

THE "PERFECT" LEADER

Many churches should ask themselves if they have the wrong understanding of what kinds of adults are best at working with youth. More churches are saying that people who work with youth should be older than most present youth workers. Some churches propose a new prerequisite for working with youth: a person has to be at least 50 years old. They suggest that it takes people of that age to have adequate substance and experiences to share with the young folks.

I can just hear it now: "Well, pastor, I'm sorry, but you're just not old enough to be working with our youth. In 10 to 15 years, if you're still interested, we may consider you."

Let's carry this thought one step further. Lists of characteristics of the "ideal" youth worker usually contain these good-sounding words:

✔listens well
✔understands youth
✔communicates well
✔has a good sense of humor
✔is a good, genuine adult model
✔is committed to the Lord
✔is fun to be with

If anything, these lists are a disservice to youth ministry. Stereotypes tend to make us feel unqualified and guilty about the gifts we don't have! It also seems apparent that most of those characteristics can be found in people over 50, just as well as in those under 50. Perhaps we need a campaign to bring the older adult church workers back into the mainstream of youth ministry.

Maybe all this leads you to consider your role in youth ministry, both now and in the future. What can you do to check out where God may want you to put your emphasis in ministry to others? Here's a checklist to consider:

List the gifts you've been given. Go on, it's good therapy. If you're really honest, you probably can come up with more gifts than you first thought.

Now place a star beside those gifts that you can use specifically in youth ministry.

Place a check mark beside those gifts that could be better used in ministry with a different age group. For example, if you would rather be spending time with the senior citizen's group, great! If your gifts and interests point toward ministry with another age group, accept that fact and consider ways to better use your gifts.

Talk regularly with someone close to you about your feelings regarding your youth ministry. Does this ministry satisfy you? Why or why not? Are you being supported and affirmed? How can you help others to be more supportive to you?

Interview and survey adults and youth around you to find how they feel about youth ministry. Do they see you only as a "temporary" youth worker? Help them share their feelings. Share your feelings with them as well.

Consider ways in which you can involve more adults in youth ministry. Help them work into various activities and plans. Work together with youth and adult planning teams. Help to bring youth and adults back together again. In so doing, perhaps you too will gain additional support and relationships with other adults in your church. See yourself as an "equipper" and not just a "doer."

Celebrate your age—whatever it is. If you can't play volleyball anymore, don't worry. The kids don't need a tall, "jock" youth leader spiking that ball at them all the time. And there's no need to prove yourself anymore. They'll like you whether or not you're athletic. Model what it means to be a 40-year-old adult.

Talk with someone close to you about your feelings. Ask them to help you think through the question, "What do I want to do with my life five years from now? 10 years from now?" Some of us may have to work after we turn 65. We still have a lot of good years left in ministry! Plan for those years.

If you need to move into a ministry outside the area of youth, go with the Lord's blessings! Your experiences in youth ministry will be extremely valuable to you in whatever ministry area you enter.

Ask kids to evaluate you. It'll keep you alert and will aid in developing a relationship with them. Find out how they feel about adults involved with them in ministry. When I was younger, some of my best teachers were in the over-50 bracket. They had something to share about life, about their subjects, about their priorities. Help kids to help you by asking for their comments and feedback.

YOUR CHOICES

So then, is youth ministry a stepping stone, a lifetime position, or something between the two? We need to remember that all ministry is full time. We also need to change attitudes that would consider the youth worker professional as someone "on the way" to somewhere else.

Youth ministry is a legitimate, lifetime, priority ministry. But it is not for everyone.

You and I can work hard at changing attitudes that attempt to dissect youth and adults from each other, as well as attitudes that put youth ministry on a lower priority scale than other ministry areas. The best way to start that change is to begin with ourselves. We can verbalize our feelings that youth ministry is not a stepping stone to bigger and greater things. However, we can also affirm professionals who for other reasons choose to move into another ministry area.

ADDITIONAL READING

If You Don't Know Where You're Going, You'll Probably End Up Somewhere Else, David Campbell, Argus.

What Color Is Your Parachute: A Practical Manual for Job Hunters and Career Changers, Richard N. Bolles, Ten Speed.

Does what happens in your
youth ministry control the
way you feel about
yourself? Here's how to
sort through doubts.

CHAPTER

32

Do You Know The Real You?

BY PAUL BORTHWICK.

Youth minister Terry is 41 years old, but he tries to look younger. He uses teenage slang, and his jokes are modeled after those he hears at the high schools he visits. Some people actually think Terry is in his early 20s, except for the receding hairline and large belly.

Joan is 25, so looking and feeling young isn't a problem. She hangs around with her youth group members at the pizza house on Saturday nights. She goes to all the high school athletic events, and she volunteers to chaperon dances. She has few friends her own age.

Rob has adult friends, and he looks adult, but he acts like the junior highers with whom he works. He often embarrasses his wife with his behavior in public. Leaders of the church often ask themselves, "Will Rob ever grow up?"

The rub in each of these people's ministries is a weak self-concept, brought on by an intense desire to be accepted by the teenagers with whom they work.

Having poor self-image is a problem we all face at one time or another in our ministry with youth. How do we feel secure enough to be ourselves with our youth? How do we build the confidence needed to be stable in our own self-images?

WHY SELF-DOUBT?

Before developing solutions for handling self-doubt, let's look at three major hazards we face as youth workers.

Age: The issue of age is a no-win situation in youth work. If we are young, parents and other adults think of us as immature and unwise. Unfortunately, we doubt any degree of effectiveness we experience with youth when someone asks why we don't have *adults* involved with the youth group.

But, those of us who are older often feel ill-equipped to work with youth because we feel out of touch. When we get the invitation to our 10th or 20th high school reunion, many of us wonder if we're fooling ourselves about being effective with youth.

When we haven't resolved the issue of age in our lives, we either resort to bizarre behavior (such as Terry and Rob) or we resign, thinking we can no longer be useful.

Performance: What is success in youth ministry? Is it having a large group? Is success a large, flashy retreat? Or is success giving the kids a good time every week?

We struggle within ourselves to be important. We know that long-term commitment to youth work is a key to effectiveness, but we wonder whether that commitment will satisfy our need for personal success. Then we compare ourselves with our peers: "What am I doing in youth work? My friends are lawyers, business executives and doctors; I work with kids. Other volunteers in the church are leading our congregation in great decisions; I can scarcely lead a retreat."

We get caught between parents, who think we're too light in our discipline, and young people, who think we're too strict. And there are friends who tease, "So, what are you going to be when you grow up?" We laugh on the outside; we collapse on the inside.

Results: Even if we accept our age and our performance in youth leadership, we still feel battered by the pressures to produce results.

"Why haven't you changed my kid yet?" It's amazing, isn't it, how some parents who've failed to communicate with their children in 15 years expect massive changes in 15 weeks? Yet our inability to perform miracles eats at us, and we question our effectiveness, our abilities and our calling.

We may want to quit. We might try to blame others. We might even ask God why he allows us to be so fruitless. All these thoughts lead us to the desperate conclusion: I am worthless. I am a failure.

WHAT YOU CAN DO

Self-image struggles are inevitable, but we can make certain changes to protect our weak spirits. The following self-image builders are within our control. We can adjust and modify them to help strengthen our ability to see ourselves as God sees us.

Find a sounding board: We need a close friend who is willing to listen to our doubts, our fears, our questions and our problems without condemnation.

In my earliest years of youth ministry, Norman was my sounding board. He never tired of hearing my complaints and my fears about youth ministry. When I wondered aloud, "Why am I doing this?" he'd help me to get God's perspective on myself and my work.

My wife, Christie, is now the sounding board in my life. She listens and responds without criticism, but she loves me enough to offer her acceptance, her well-timed rebukes and her affirmation.

Without such friends, I doubt if I would have stayed in youth ministry. They have been God's messengers, sent to help me recognize the good that he is doing in and through me. They also have kicked me in the pants when I have been tempted to wallow in self-pity. Their words have strengthened my ability to understand how God sees me.

Develop outside interests: Youth work can gobble up all our time. Without exercising caution, we can find ourselves at the end of each week with no time for rest or for regeneration.

Having a healthy self-image requires that we have some outside-of-the-youth-group interests. We need to pursue interests in sports, arts, music or special hobbies so we can be deeper and broader people. You may respond, "But I can't see how going to the opera will make me a better youth leader." But being a great youth leader isn't the only reason for living. Outside interests can help us grow in our perspective on life and deliver us from the narrow-sighted "the-youth-group-is-all-that-matters" approach.

Some youth leaders take up photography, playing the piano or whale watching. (The last one might be difficult if you live in Iowa.) My wife and I have developed an interest in bird watching. While it is unrelated to youth ministry, bird watching helps us to realize that God's world is bigger than our youth group.

Allow for depression: There will be times in youth ministry when our self-doubt, negative feelings and sense of worthlessness will peak. It may be, for some, in the middle of winter. For instance, it may come after someone criticizes the ministry. Depression may even strike after an immensely successful youth event.

Knowing ourselves and being honest about these down times is the first place to start. During these times, we may need to retreat to cultivate our relationship with God. We might need the counsel of our sounding-board person. We might just need a meal and a good night's sleep (such as Elijah in 1 Kings 19).

While we shouldn't indulge ourselves with self-pity, we have to allow for the times when our feelings are low. God can speak to us in these times, but this will happen only when we realize that it's okay to come to him in the midst of our fears and insecurities.

Go outside your ministry: A healthy sense of self-worth requires that we recognize we're not alone in youth ministry. By visiting other youth groups, we can discover the strengths and weaknesses of our ministries and our leadership styles. This, in turn, can help us to see our group's uniquenesses.

When discouraged youth leaders visit my youth group, they sometimes ask: "Do you mean that you have problems with cliques too? You have problems getting group members to sing? Your group feels bored and apathetic sometimes too?" They probably thought their groups' problems were unique. They probably felt isolated and like a failure, until they realized their struggles were typical.

Going outside of our groups can show us where we are succeeding, where we need to grow, but, best of all, it can reassure us that we are not alone.

Develop a team: We need the body of Christ to realize a personal sense of worth and uniqueness and to grow in our ability to accept ourselves. We need a youth ministry team, a group of co-workers who share the leadership load.

A youth leadership team, if characterized by love, honesty and sensitivity, can enable every member of the team to be free to utilize gifts and abilities to the maximum. The team can free up the older members to be the respected sages and the younger members to be their enthusiastic selves. The team can protect us from criticism, and it can be the source of strength we need when endurance is hard to come by.

Jack, 21, who is on our youth ministry team, recently was criticized by parents for being immature and irresponsible. He was devastated and wanted to quit the team. Through the youth ministry team's support, Jack changed his mind. The team helped him to see through the parent's criticism to the struggles they themselves were having with their teenagers. With honest love, the team encouraged Jack to be more responsible, but it also helped Jack accept the fact that at age 21 he wasn't as mature as 45-year-old parents expected him to be.

Grow in relationship with God: To base how we feel about ourselves on things that shift and change (such as success, others' opinions of us or our age) is asking for trouble. We need a solid foundation on which to build our view of ourselves. That foundation is God.

When we maintain this relationship as top priority, we find that God's opinion of us matters more than criticism. When we feel inadequate because of our age, God can comfort us. When performance pressures mount, we can remember that God sees accomplishments that remain unseen to others. When lack of results bogs us down, we can remember that God asks us to be faithful, not successful.

Through our relationships with God, our partnership with others, and our own personal growth, we can develop peace and confidence in ourselves and in the work to which God has directed us.

ADDITIONAL READING

Passages: Predictable Crises of Adult Life, Gail Sheehy, Dutton.

How you feel about
yourself need not depend
on the ups and downs of
your ministry. Take time
now to review your
thought patterns.

CHAPTER

33

Self-Esteem And Success: Evaluating Values

BY DAVID R. HELMS

In the best seller **Your Erroneous Zones**, Dr. Wayne Dyer discusses the variety of irrational thoughts, beliefs and thinking patterns that many people accept as truth. He explains that these self-defeating behavioral patterns blind people to reality, rob them of energy and vitality and, if left unchecked, can lead to serious neuroses or worse.

As I considered my years in youth ministry, I realized I had allowed a tremendously erroneous (i.e., untrue; not based on reality or fact) idea to develop and dominate my thinking: *I felt my self-worth was synonymous with my success as a youth minister.* This value system seemed to work fine for several years—until my youth ministry "empire" (my alter ego) began to slowly decline, according to my standards of success. Then I got increasingly frustrated, irritable, depressed and generally unhappy with myself, my work and other people.

I did notice, however, that I was in good company. I saw that other youth ministers also had confused their personal worth with their success as ministers of youth. As I said, this faulty way of thinking does "work well" when attendance is up and your popularity with the youth and their parents is secure. But beware when things aren't going so well! Then youth ministers ask self-defeating questions such as, "What's the matter with me?" or, worse yet, "God, what am I doing wrong, and why have you forsaken me?"

If you identify with these erroneous, self-defeating thought patterns, here are some suggestions for you:

- Admit that you have a problem and ask God to help you.
- Develop positive self-esteem habits. Say to yourself: "My worth as a person does not depend on what I do or what I accomplish. God called me to youth ministry before I had proven anything and he continues to accept me on that basis."
- Determine or re-establish your personal priorities. Make a list.
- Schedule time for yourself and regularly use it to do something that's important to you.
- Schedule time to spend with someone who's special to you—your spouse or close friend.
- If you have definite days off, take them.
- Develop friendships away from the church community so that you build an identity that isn't associated with the church.
- Work again on a hobby or skill that you enjoyed during school years.
- Find a new hobby or interest and schedule time for it on a regular basis.
- Join a community organization.

When you follow these suggestions, there are no guarantees that your youth ministry "empire" will take a turn for the better. But your erroneous moans about your self-worth will disappear when you see yourself as a distinct person separate from your ministry.

And remember, as the late Rev. Grady Nutt pointed out, "God told Jesus, 'This is my beloved Son in whom I am well pleased' at the *beginning* of Jesus' ministry—not after it was completed."

ADDITIONAL READING

The Success Fantasy, Anthony Campolo, Victor.
Your Erroneous Zones, Wayne Dyer, Avon.

Quality? Quantity? What
is the measuring rod
of your group? Use these
standards to assess
your efforts.

CHAPTER

34

Three Ways Of Evaluating Ministry Success

BY JIM HANCOCK

I t's been suggested that if we youth workers were paid on a commission basis, we'd reach a lot more kids. That's a provocative and, unless you're a youth worker, humorous notion. If you think competition is stiff now between First Church and Second Church, wait until the youth pastors are going after grocery money. But is that the point? Do full Sunday school classes and big retreats tell the story?

Perhaps. But, perhaps not.

Another school of youth ministry motivation suggests that it is the quality of the product that proves the ministry's worth.

"We've only got a few," the senior pastor beams to his colleagues at the ministerial association, "but they're disciples!"

Across the table another pastor is thinking: *"Yep, I hear that. We've only got a few, but boy are they dead."*

Whether or not you're on the winning end of the quality game you've got to answer the question, "What have we produced and at what expense?"

And so the arguments go. Quantity? Quality? Can we have both? Or maybe a blend of the two: a lot of not-bad-if-you-don't-look-too-closely Christian kids.

The criteria for success are complicated.

SOME BASICS

Difficult though it may be, it is possible to isolate characteristics of a successful youth ministry. We're not talking about a particular philosophy of ministry here. There are several, apparently successful, approaches to youth work.

Here are three standards by which to evaluate success: 1. Program success. 2. Interpersonal success. 3. Personal success.

Program success. One evidence of success is the production of programs to which kids come. You can argue that programming is secondary to relationships, but you'll get strong argument back on two counts.

First, we'd like to know what you have to offer the kids you meet, for that matter, so would they. How many relationships can you sustain without effective programs?

Second, your board would like to know how your work fits into the larger church picture. What are the evidences that your presence makes a difference in the church?

Crisp, fresh programs gain us access to kids we'll never meet any other way. Good programming also helps us hang on to kids when there are so many of them around that intimacy becomes difficult. The youth worker who fails to pay attention to the programming can't succeed.

But what makes for a successful program? That depends on what you're trying to accomplish. Some programs are solely for the purpose of gathering students, some for teaching, some to produce fellowship, some just for fun. Measure the success of a program by what it is designed to do.

Ideally, our programs should cover the dual functions of expanding and deepening the church's influence. Some programs, typically Sunday school and Bible studies, help deepen the people who are in the church. Other programs (here the strategies are nearly endless) can be designed to be doors through which people can enter.

Interpersonal success. A concerned parent eyes us nervously across the desk. She shifts uncomfortably in her chair. So do we.

"I appreciate all you're doing," she says cautiously. "I hear that wonderful things are going on. It's just that (we can hear it coming) my Tommy doesn't seem to fit in . . . "

So you've got the best program in town. So you've got a detailed plan that begins the day a youngster enters your territory and carries through month by month until he or she exits the other side. What do you do with the ones who don't fit in? Refer them to another church?

The way in which we deal with people plays an important part in determining success or failure in ministry. If we're so oriented to programs that we can't see human need, can't respond to the kid who's not a "typical teenager," then we can't succeed. If we've alienated parents, staff, volunteers and kids, we're in for tough going

The most misplaced youth workers I know are men and women who don't really like kids. What they are doing in youth ministry has little to do with nurturing young Christians.

The second most misplaced youth workers are those who don't like parents. They aren't simply frustrated and discouraged about moms and dads. They see parents as the enemy, as obstacles to be surmounted, problems to be solved.

The third most misplaced youth workers are those who will not be supervised. They are so filled with self-importance that anyone who offers help or direction is threatening.

Such misplaced ministers seldom last long on the job. Not because they fail at tasks, but because they fail in relationships. The good news is that healthy relationships can nurse us through tough times in other areas. When the programs are not yet demonstrating their potentials, when we've tried and failed, the people around us—kids, parents, fellow staff—will support us if they know us and trust us.

Personal success. A close friend was asked what he'd like to tell youth workers. His wry response: "How to write a good resume'."

Youth ministry is a revolving-door profession. You've probably heard, depending on your source, that the average stay in a youth position is somewhere between nine and 18 months. Even on the liberal end those numbers are discouraging and they imply a great deal of frustration.

Lack of program and interpersonal success affects tenure.
So does the absence of personal success. It is possible to
have had a going ministry with kids yet still leave feeling
drained and dissatisfied.

What are the components of personal success? They include what we've already discussed. The knowledge that we
are doing a good job and that our relationships are in good
order goes far toward personal satisfaction. But there's
more. It is within the realm of reason to experience personal
success even when program success is not yet evident.

Most of us have offered the wisdom of Luke to the young-
sters. Let's take advantage of it for ourselves.

"And Jesus grew in *wisdom* and *stature* and in favor with
God and *man*" (Luke 2:52).

Personal success depends on growth in these areas: intellectual, physical, spiritual and social. A look at last week's
schedule can tell us a lot about how responsibly we're handling this biblical passage. It may be necessary to set specific priorities and to assign time in the week for each of
these. If that's what it takes, we'd better be tough-minded
enough to do it.

Here are some other areas to consider:

● Am I spending an appropriate amount and quality of
time with my family or intimate friends?

● Am I being stretched beyond what I know I can do
apart from God's intervention?

● Is there adventure in my life? Am I taking risks?

● Am I having fun?

● Am I walking with God? What evidence is there of that?

Bedrock of success. Did you ever rush out of your office
and into the hall and then wonder why you were there?
That's how a lot of us do youth ministry. The process swal-
lows up the direction.

"I do this because it works this way. And I know it works
this way, otherwise why would I be doing it?" The process
looks good on paper, but we're left wondering why we're
here. We have motion but we lack goals.

If we're to be successful in youth ministry, we must aim
at something specific. We need somewhere to go. We've got
to have well-defined, attainable, measurable goals.

But whose goals? Our own? The church's? God's?
All the above.

Successful Leadership Traits

Leadership traits can be difficult to pin down, but following is a list of attributes gathered from various sources.

A good leader:

● knows how to focus his or her energy and talents on the relevant aspects of a challenge or problem.

● is able to work at understanding a situation or problem before making a judgment.

● observes and absorbs situations to see what really exists, rather than the way it appears.

● plans the use of time wisely and skillfully.

● sets specific goals and uses most of his or her energy to solve problems and deal with situations that impede progress toward those goals.

● builds on his or her strengths and seeks to minimize weaknesses.

● knows how to ask clear and concise questions.

● welcomes new and challenging ideas, even concepts that question or conflict with his or her point of view.

● urges others to offer diverse opinions on the topic or situation.

● is open, sensitive, encouraging and responsive.

● considers others as more important than himself or herself.

● knows how to listen to others.

● takes notes and jots down thoughts for future use.

—*Gary Richardson*

Of course we begin by considering God's goals for our work. What he demands of us we demand of ourselves. What God allows, we allow. What he forbids us, we forbid ourselves.

We next take account of the church's goals. This is no place to spiritualize. Every church has goals, whether formal or informal. Part of our job is to discern those goals and to do what we can to fit into the total picture.

There remain personal goals. What are the elements of style you'd like to bring to the youth ministry? How long would you like to stay? If you leave, what would you like to leave behind?

Goal success is measured by the extent to which we incorporate God's will, the church's will and our own will into the work we do. It is also measured by our movement from elementary to secondary goals; from the "let's get 'em here" level to the "let's do something with them" level, and so on.

One reason for the high turnover in youth positions is that most of us maintain a shallow reservoir of goals. A year into the job we've done almost everything we know to do. Eight-

een months along we're serving leftovers. Two years and
we're long gone.

Time is an important factor in the process toward reaching the goals you set. It takes two years to get rolling in a
particular ministry setting: a year to get one foot on the
ground, a year to get the other foot down. Then you can begin running. Those first two years are tedious, low-profile
work. The fun begins once the foundational work is done.
Unfortunately, most youth workers never get that far.

For those who do, youth work can be a lifelong ministry of
satisfaction and success.

ADDITIONAL READING

Management, Peter F. Drucker, Harper and Row.
Seeds of Greatness, Denis Waitley, Revell.

Like a slow-acting poison, unjustified criticism can destroy you. Here are 10 antidotes when you're the victim or verbal attacks.

You Can Learn To Grow From Unfair Criticism

BY JOHN CASSIS

Everyone has experienced criticism. To be involved in ministry to and with others is to be criticized. Criticism hurts. "It's like standing helpless in front of a frenzied mob and letting them slash and cut at you with knives," admits one youth leader, who had been unjustly criticized for her handling of a youth group problem.

Even though it hurts, most of us will admit that criticism—if it is constructive—can be quite good for us. It can make us better persons. Better Christians.

A proverb says it beautifully: "If you profit from constructive criticism, you shall be elected to the wise man's hall of fame" (Proverbs 15:31). It goes on to say, "But to reject constructive criticism is to harm yourself." Then you're not looking out for your own best interests.

We want to grow in our relationships with others, so we need to learn how to cope with criticism. But sometimes we reject criticism because it's destructive or it comes across in an angry or vengeful way. Other times we simply don't like to look honestly at ourselves. We're blind to our faults.

In either case, what can you do when you receive any kind of criticism? Here are 10 statements to consider.

SAY IT—WEIGH IT

When you first hear the criticism, repeat it aloud to the critic. This not only assures understanding, but prevents you from getting impatient and defensive. Someone said, "Patience is the ability to let your light shine after your fuse has blown!" How true.

Then weigh the criticism. Ask yourself if there is any truth to the statement. Take an honest look at yourself. If the criticism is valid, take correcting actions. Make necessary changes.

However, if the criticism isn't valid, if it is unfair, if it is destructive, then forget it. A church I pastored once asked me to attract more young people to the services. To accomplish this, I decided to complement our 18th century hymnal with a contemporary youth hymnal. In the Sunday morning services we sang two older, more traditional hymns then one newer, more contemporary song arranged for guitars, horns and drums to give more life to the music. More and more young people began to attend church. Enthusiasm spread throughout the youth group. Then I received a stinging letter from a person who wrote: "You've ruined the worship service! Those contemporary hymnals have got to go—or I will leave!" Although in the minority, this person wasn't alone. I had to make a decision. I weighed the criticism and the consequences, and I realized that too many young people were coming to church and becoming Christians to stop. I tried to reconcile the relationship with those who were displeased, but it did not work. A few families left the church, but the church continued its solid growth. Weigh the criticism. Then decide.

PLAY IT DOWN—PRAY IT UP

Once you weigh the criticism, play it down and pray about it! Instead of repeatedly turning it over in your mind, turn it over to God. A key verse is Philippians 4:6—"Do not be anxious about anything, but in everything, by prayer and petition, with thanksgiving, present your requests to God."

DON'T LOOK BACK

A crucial part of making a great comeback after being

crushed is not to look back. Forget the destructive remarks. The Apostle Paul on death row in a damp, dirty Roman prison wrote, "Forgetting what lies behind and straining forward to what lies ahead, I press on for the upward calling of Christ Jesus" (Philippians 3:13-14).

A friend of mine once said, "You don't drown when you fall into the water, you only drown when you stay there!" Those who consciously or unconsciously attack you can only drown you when you choose to stay in the sinking, stinking waters of criticism.

CRITICISM FROM LITTLE MINDS IS WORTH LITTLE

The Apostle Paul, who faced constant criticism in his ministry, said it well, "It is a very small thing that I should be judged by you" (1 Corinthians 4:3).

Ask yourself: "Is my main purpose to please God or to please others?"

We will always pay a price for the responsibility we assume as leaders. As someone has said, "The higher you climb the ladder, the more your rear is exposed." If pleasing God becomes most important in your life, then you can build a resistance to those destructive forces that try to pull you down.

KITES RISE HIGHEST AGAINST THE WIND

During the rough years of World War II, Winston Churchill wrote, "Kites rise highest against the wind." If you are courageous through the tough times, then you will find yourself reaching new heights, new potentials and new strengths.

Jesus said: "Blessed are you when men revile you and persecute you and utter all kinds of evil against you falsely on my account. Rejoice and be glad, for your reward is great in heaven" (Matthew 5:11-12).

YOU ARE SPECIAL TO GOD

When the weight of criticism begins to sink your self-worth, you must remember you are special to your fantastic Father in heaven. Criticism is a form of rejection, and there is no rejection that can ever separate you from his love.

Mary Crowley, a successful Christian businesswoman, says, "We are all somebodies, because the almighty God doesn't take time to create nobodies."

GO BEYOND UGLY NATURES; SEE URGENT NEEDS

Jesus had the ability to look beyond people's ugly natures and see their urgent needs. When someone has leveled unjust criticism toward you, it helps to live the kind of loving that Jesus was all about. People with acid tongues desperately need to be loved, accepted and forgiven. Your forgiveness could be the power that frees them from their negative prisons. Remember, allow others the right to be inconsistent in their actions and words, just as you allow yourself that right to be inconsistent.

PRACTICE A POSITIVE ATTITUDE

"Whatever is true, whatever is honorable, whatever is just, whatever is pure, whatever is lovely, whatever is gracious, if there is any excellence, if there is anything worthy of praise, think about these things!" (Philippians 4:8).

CRITICISM ONLY HURTS IF YOU LET IT

Booker T. Washington, ex-slave who founded Tuskegee Institute at a time when racial prejudice was at its peak, said, "I will permit no man to narrow and degrade my soul by making me hate him."

We choose what we believe or disbelieve. We choose to let criticism hurt us, or not hurt us.

FORGIVENESS IS THE KEY

The ultimate way to cope with criticism is illustrated by our Lord: Forgiveness. Read Mark 15 for a look at the terrible forms of criticism Jesus experienced in the last few hours of his life. The Roman soldiers mocked him, put a crown of thorns on his head, laughed at him, beat him, hanged him on a cross and taunted him. On the cross, even a smelly thief rejected Jesus. But in that moment, Jesus said, "Father, forgive them, for they don't know what they're doing."

God expects the same reaction from us.

ADDITIONAL READING

Coping With Difficult People, Robert M. Bramson, Doubleday.

Creative Conflict, Richard L. Krebs, Augsburg.

Creative Suffering, Paul Tournier, Harper and Row.

The success of our work
in ministry depends a great
deal on how well we
communicate.

CHAPTER
36

Three Ideas To Help You Be a Better Speaker

BY KEN DAVIS

Believe it or not, it's possible to have graduated from an excellent seminary with top-notch grades in homiletics, to be in charge of the largest youth program in history, yet be a poor communicator. I have listened to enough boring sermons, devotionals, raps, and even "motivational" talks to realize that effective communication goes beyond what is covered in the textbooks.

The good speaker makes the audience *want* to listen. The good speaker paves a road of entertainment, humor, fact and fancy—then leads the audience down that road to truth.

Even if you can't recognize an outline when you see one, I believe the following practical steps can help you communicate more effectively.

WHEREVER YOU GO, TAKE A NOTEBOOK

The whole world is your resource. The most effective speakers make good use of that resource. They spice their talks with observations taken from everyday life. These everyday experiences, ideas, quotes and illustrations are the jewels that distinguish between a mediocre speaker and an excellent communicator.

For example, several months ago I answered the doorbell and was greeted by a little girl, her blonde hair in a pony-tail, who was selling Girl Scout cookies. In a sweet little voice she told me that by buying her cookies, I could do three things at once: help her win a prize, support the Girl Scouts, and become the proud owner of some of the finest cookies in the world. The little girl had her sales presentation down pat, but there was one major problem. My 10-year-old daughter was standing at my elbow reminding me that people had been finding needles, pins and other difficult-to-digest objects in Girl Scout cookies. I kindly declined the sales pitch.

That should have been the end of it. The little salesperson turned to leave. Then as if an idea had just struck her, she quickly turned to me, her eyes sparkling with hope. She looked directly into my eyes and said, "You know what?" With shaky hands she opened a box of cookies and tore the cellophane from one of the packages. She carefully broke a cookie into quarters, explaining that if I did this before I ate any I could be sure they were safe. With a new burst of insight, she added, "If you find anything bad in the cookies, I'll buy them all back." I bought $50 worth of cookies. I guess I'm a sucker for a good sales pitch.

But I didn't realize just how much of a sucker until two days later. My family and I were at a neighbor's home enjoying a quiet dinner when the doorbell rang. From where I was sitting, I could see it was the same little cookie seller I had met earlier. My friend quickly explained that she had seen the publicity about Girl Scout cookies and didn't care to buy any. The little girl sadly turned away, and then, as if an idea had just struck her, she turned back, her eyes sparkling with hope, and said, "You know what?"

I was incredulous as I watched the little genius sell $25 worth of cookies to my friend.

What a great illustration! This experience had that special feel. I took the time to carefully write it down. Recently while preparing a speech for a group of sales executives, I came across my notes in my files. It fit perfectly with the theme of my address.

Keep a notepad or tape recorder by your bed. Some of

your greatest ideas will come as you lie waiting to go to sleep. Turn on the light and record the ideas in detail. Unless you do, in the morning the inspiration will be gone.

When you watch television, have a notebook in your lap and a pencil in your hand. Dozens of useful ideas will flit through your mind. These random ideas not only help you communicate better, but also can enrich activities and programming.

During the day, learn to actually *see* what goes on around you. Don't look only for things that fit into a talk you are preparing. If an experience touches you, make a note of it and file it away. Someday it may be your best illustration.

TARGET THE PURPOSE OF EACH TALK

Once while hunting deer in northern Minnesota, I heard a shot ring out. The bullet came so close I could feel the percussion from its passage. My mind made a mental note of how close that must have been, and I continued walking. A few seconds later I heard another shot. This time the bullet hit a tree next to my face. Again my mind noted that the bullet had come awfully close. When a third shot broke a branch just inches from my nose, I suddenly concluded that someone was shooting at me, and I dived for the ground.

As I hit the dirt (not to be confused with biting the dust), a man emptied his rifle in my direction. He had never seen me; he was simply shooting at sounds. Evidently his theory was: There are deer in there somewhere; and if I shoot enough lead into the woods, I might get one.

What an inefficient and dangerous way to hunt! Yet I have heard dozens of speakers who apparently have the same philosophy: If I just talk long enough, I'm bound to communicate something. A hunter will only be successful if he knows exactly what he's after, takes aim at that single target, and excludes all distractions.

Likewise with speakers. One of the most valuable pieces of advice ever given to me was: If you can't write what you're trying to say in a single sentence, then you're trying to say too much.

When preparing for this assignment, I had many aspects of communication I wanted to write about, but I couldn't get them to fit in a single simple sentence. I finally wrote, "My purpose is to help my readers give better talks." I narrowed it down even further by adding *how* I wished to accomplish that goal: "By revealing what I believe are the three *most* important steps." Now my purpose was specific: Help you give betters talks. And my method was absolutely clear: Share the three most important steps to make that possible.

Following is an example of a bad purpose statement:

My purpose tonight is to tell my group members about God and all the good things he has done for us by using the Bible as my source.

I'll guarantee this is going to be a vague and boring talk. You could spend a lifetime on that subject—it's too broad. A better approach would be:

My purpose tonight is to teach my group members that God is good. I will do this by sharing scripture verses that deal with his goodness, by giving my personal testimony of his goodness and by making them aware of the good things he has done in their lives.

Here we have a single purpose supported by three points. Close inspection reveals, however, that this talk could be simplified even more:

My purpose tonight is to reveal to group members how God has been good to me, by sharing three personal experiences of his goodness in my life.

The human mind can remain at attention for only a short time. If your time is spent focused on a narrow band of truth and your illustrations, humor and facts all point in that same direction, then your audience will receive and retain much more of what you say. And they'll also enjoy it more.

TAPE EVERY TALK YOU GIVE

I set a small tape recorder where it will pick up my voice as I give my talk. I then listen to the tape as soon as possible. I was amazed at what I learned the first time I did this. I used poor grammar throughout, and I started two stories that I never finished!

It is even better to videotape one of your presentations. You will see yourself exactly as the audience sees you. It's shocking. I discovered upon viewing a tape of myself that I spoke to only one side of the audience. Not once during a 30-minute talk did I ever establish eye contact with anyone on the left side of that room. These taping exercises provide instant information on your performance and allow the opportunity to adjust, improve and then take another look.

As leaders we dare not stop improving in every area of our lives. The success of our work depends a great deal on how well we communicate. Also—the message we are trying to communicate *demands* the best we can give.

I challenge you for 90 days to:

1. Carry a notebook and write down all those wonderful ideas and experiences that have been slipping your mind.

2. Prepare every talk with a single focus that can be expressed in a simple sentence.

3. Tape every talk you give so you can listen and learn.

I guarantee you will become a more effective communicator. You will hear the improvement yourself. But, most importantly, those to whom you speak will hear it too.

Talking Too Much

A lot of youth workers believe that their speeches are single-handedly keeping kids' interest, catalyzing life-long changes, etc.

Baloney.

In fact, a lot of talking often produces little learning, concludes John Goodlad, dean of education at the University of California at Los Angeles.

Goodlad conducted an eight-year nationwide study of America's school problems and determined that teachers talk too much and bore their students. Teachers should emphasize active participation, says Goodlad. For example, a lesson on "Jonah and the Whale" might have young people experience time alone in silence and darkness.

This study suggests that young people in youth groups, as in classrooms, learn more by doing than by listening. In other words, the better speaker knows when to stop talking and start facilitating active learning experiences.

ADDITIONAL READING

Caring Enough to Hear and Be Heard, David Augsburger, Herald.

The Miracle of Dialogue, Reuel Howe, Winston-Seabury.

Storytelling: The Enchantment of Theology, Belden C. Lane, Christian Board of Publication.

Unlock your abilities
and potentials. Find out
how to free and rekindle
the imaginative person
inside you.

CHAPTER

37

Unwrap Your Creative Gifts

BY CHARLES BRADSHAW

An old frame church in New England stood in such desperate need of exterior paint that the minister recruited a half-dozen volunteers from his congregation. But he couldn't get them to show up for the job, that is, until he had a devilish inspiration. He divided the building into six segments. Then, in bold letters three feet high, he painted a volunteer's name on each segment. Shortly thereafter each recruit dutifully arrived to paint his segment, fulfill the pledge, and avoid public notoriety.

We've all met people with an uncanny ability to be creative. We wonder how they do it. *Creative* is an exciting word. When we hear it mentioned, most of us think wistfully of someone else with that gift of freshness and spontaneity.

Often those of us who work with youth wish we could be more creative, but are sure that is impossible. One of the most persistent and widespread myths about creativity is that it's the exclusive property of a few talented people.

An impressive body of solid research over the past few decades proves that creative ability is almost universally distributed. There's also ample proof that creativity can be rekindled in those whose potential creativity is buried under layers of personal and environmental barriers and suppressions.

BLOCKS OF CREATIVITY

Most of us have plenty of creative potential bottled up inside waiting to get out. Few people lack creativity, but too many of us in the church feel our ducts have been blocked. Do any of the following obstructions to creativity fit you?

Self-discouragement. "I had a creative idea once, but I suggested it to the committee and ... " Most of us have had a creative idea shot down by a committee. Creativity is a fragile gift.

Remember, first tries are seldom successful. Perhaps only one out of 10 creative ideas blossoms into a workable program. But think of the beautiful fragrance of the one that does.

Fear. There are countless opportunities for failure, but few of them carry stiff penalties. However, most of us seem to wait until we either "know it all" or feel comfortably secure before we speak or act upon a situation.

The fear of looking foolish is an all-too-common emotional block. Dr. James Bryant Conant White, president of Harvard University, kept on his office wall a drawing of a turtle with this motto: Behold the turtle. He makes progress only when his neck is out.

Fear deters creativity through misdirecting our energy and by keeping us from the action necessary to its development.

Doubting your ability. In his book, **The Making of a Christian Leader**, Ted Engstrom points out that the key to creativity lies within the leader's own personality. A *healthy* view of yourself, your relationship with God and others, and your belief in the work God has called you to do combine to make you capable of creative thinking.

Ego strength is not an ego trip. A belief in your ability is not a license to become a blowhard. It is simply a necessary trait for the further development of creative behavior. Begin to believe in your own creative potential, and you will begin to be more creative. It is a requisite attitude to creative growth. You can do it. Let the juices flow.

DEVELOP YOUR CREATIVE POTENTIAL

Walt Disney advised us to look on our imaginations as mental muscles. We can let our creative gift shrivel through disuse. Take on those activities which are most likely to provide our imaginations with exercise. Thus, creative power "can actually be stimulated into growth," according to Professor H.A. Overstreet.

Feed your imagination. To develop creativity, the mind needs not only to be exercised but to be filled with material out of which ideas can best be formed. The richest fuel for ideation and creativity is experience. Firsthand experience provides the richest fuel, since it is more apt to stay with us and bubble up when needed. Secondhand experience such as reading, listening or merely being a spectator, provides for thinner fuel.

Travel also feeds imagination. The high spots linger long in our memories and strengthen our power of association. Whether the travel is "out of this world" or into the suburbs, it does add to our experience.

Read actively. Francis Bacon declared, "Reading maketh a full man." Reading supplies bread for imagination to feed upon. Our imaginations are sparked by the right kind of reading:

● According to Harry Emerson Fosdick, "The most rewarding form of reading is biography." Any life worth publishing usually reveals an inspiring record of ideation.

● Short stories are short mainly because they leave so much to the imagination. Try to outwit the author by reading the first half of the story, then thinking up your own outline for the second half.

● The Bible is a source of creative development for those who read actively and with alertness.

Read actively. Test yourself. Read one paragraph of the Bible. Close it. Tell yourself out loud what you read.

Take time to read, but not just religious or youth ministry books. Read outside your field. Don't just read what you agree with. Ask others what they are reading. Develop new interests. A refreshing time for me in my graduate studies was the reading of 80 children's books for a literature course. Years later, I'm still drawing ideas from those books as well as making recommendations to parents and children alike.

CULTIVATING YOUR CREATIVITY

Activities are tools for developing creativity. Try one:

1. Try turning your gripes into plans for action. Make notes of the next five "discontents" you find yourself mentioning. Then at a later time try to find 20 different ways for resolving each dissatisfaction.

2. Play the old "close your eyes and guess what this is" game. Have someone blindfold you and put 10 items in front of you to identify by touch alone. Try to discover the cause of five unfamiliar sounds in the distance.

3. Try writing your name by placing a pen between your toes. You should immediately become aware of how children learn through their sense of touch.

4. Without speaking or writing, attempt to describe the essence of your belief in Christ.

5. Decide on a way to accomplish a routine task that will make the work more stimulating, or, at least, less unpleasant.

6. Plan your next youth meeting with the goal of meeting the needs of a particular young person.

Practice, practice, practice. Like jogging or speaking a new language, thinking creatively feels awkward until habits have been unlearned. To help develop creativity, try some of the following exercises:

● Write three-word phrases beginning with each letter of the alphabet. For example, "Buy better bargains."

● Make a list of five blue foods, 15 ways to use a feather or six new names for the Sunday evening youth meeting.

● Go outside your house. Look at your neighborhood as though you were seeing it for the first time. List things you haven't observed in months.

● Think of at least one way to make your surroundings more attractive or useful.

The more consistently you behave in ways which encourage creativity, the more likely you are to be creative.

Let the creative juices flow. Being creative takes more than new experiences and practice. It also takes time and a conscious effort. Alex F. Osborn, the father of modern creative thought, writes, "Every person can become a more creative person by taking time to imagine, to risk, and to dream."

Creativity takes time—time to dream. Time management expert Alan Lakein emphasizes the need to achieve a balance between quiet time and activity. A simple way to enhance creativity is to take a walk. Since the days of Thoreau, hiking has been accepted as an aid to ideation. Discipline yourself so you can take extra time to think about where you want yourself, your church, and your youth group to be in the future.

You can't force creativity. The juices don't always flow on schedule. So don't get discouraged. Creative thoughts often come when you least expect them. Keep paper and a pencil handy at all times for when the ideas come. A note pad by your bed can capture ideas that will be long gone by sunrise.

Group brainstorming for ideas can be quite productive. Often when your creative energy is low, others can rejuvenate your creative juices. The group must encourage the use of unconstrained thought. The wilder the idea, the better. The greater the number of ideas, the more the likelihood of winners.

There is a cost for creativity. Its cost is time, effort and sometimes money. But the results are worth the investment.

ADDITIONAL READING
Conceptual Blockbusting: A Guide to Better Ideas, second edition, James L. Adams, Norton.

Thinking Better, David Lewis and James Greene, Rawson-Wade.

> The church is the most
> creative gathering on
> earth. It is our responsibil-
> ity to use the gifts God has
> given us.

Develop the Creative Enabler Already Within You

BY DENNIS C. BENSON AND BILL WOLFE

S ome terms have a bad reputation. The term "creative" has become an elitist label. Creativity really has nothing to do with particular skills. While it is true that this sensitivity does include finely honed abilities, creativity is something deeper. It is the capacity to make something new, something meaningful from life's different fragments. In other words, the new is not really new. The great artist or musician does not invent the colors or the notes. He or she is able to weave the existing pieces into a new pattern. The person with this kind of vision is a creative person.

People of faith should have a special sensitivity for this kind of creativity. We are a people of the Spirit. There is a wholeness to our perspective of creation. It all comes together because God put it together. The sad reality is that most Christians don't think they are creative. Many youth workers don't consider themselves creative persons.

If we are a new creation in Christ, then the old, broken way has passed. The new has come. It is our responsibility to live out this wholeness.

One of the important things we learn from living this life of reconciliation is that we do not work alone. All creativity comes out of community in order to go back into community. All the great artists sought the community of ideas and stimulation in order to have more pieces of existence. The moment of writing, composing or organizing that youth program may be a singular task. However, we bring to that moment all the collective contributions of the community.

Unfortunately, many people in local leadership undertake their church task in the Lone Ranger model. They wonder why they soon break down. No one can be creative without the community of others. This means that the youth worker must draw upon the resources of the community. If you are the only person or a lone couple doing the job, find a few kindred spirits to put you into the creative covenant with someone else in the area. Meet a couple of times a month and share ideas. Debrief on your failures and successes.

The church is the most creative gathering on earth. Where else could you join one week and be leading a youth group the next? If you do a decent job, they will probably love what you do. If people don't support your creative ideas, it is either an inappropriate idea or they don't understand you.

YES, BUT . . .
You are a creative enabler.
  Yes, but . . . I don't have time.
You are a creative enabler.
  Yes, but . . . I don't have the experience.
You are a creative enabler.
  Yes, but . . . I don't have the equipment.
You are a creative enabler.
  Yes, but . . . I don't have the resources.
You are a creative enabler.
  Yes, but . . . I am more interested in "content."
You are a creative enabler.
  Yes, but . . . I need clear directions and guidance to teach.
You are a creative enabler.
  Yes, but . . . my kids are too unruly in class to do anything different.
You are a creative enabler.
  Yes, but . . . I will try something different later on in the

year.

You are a creative enabler.

Yes, but ... I don't have any special skills like music or art.

You are a creative enabler.

Yes, but ... my people don't go for tricky approaches to learning.

You are a creative enabler.

Yes, but ... I need help to do these kinds of things.

You are a creative enabler.

Yes, but ... our classroom facilities are not right for such things.

You are a creative enabler.

Yes, but ... it is too hard to prepare for such things.

You are a creative enabler.

Yes, but ... I was satisfied as a child with the "old-fashioned" forms of teaching.

You are a creative enabler.

Yes, but ... I might fail if I try different ways to do my teaching.

You are a creative enabler.

Yes, but ... other teachers might make fun of me.

You are a creative enabler.

Yes, but ... I am too old for changing my ways.

You are a creative enabler.

Yes, but ... I might offend Mrs. Jones.

You are a creative enabler.

Yes, but ... I am afraid.

You are a creative enabler.

Yes, but ... I am only one person.

You are a creative enabler.

Yes, but ... I am lazy and comfortable with my old approaches.

YES.

(Reprinted from **The Basic Encyclopedia for Youth Ministry**, copyright ©1981 by Dennis C. Benson and Bill Wolfe, published by Group Books.)

ADDITIONAL READING

The Courage to Create, Rollo May, Norton.

A Whack on the Side of the Head: How to Unlock Your Mind for Innovation, Roger von Oech, Warner.

Youth ministers who think
they know everything?
Pity. Especially pity
the teenagers with whom
they interact.

CHAPTER
39

Leaders Who 'Know It All' Cause Great Harm

BY JOHN SHAW

I meet a lot of different kinds of youth sponsors and ministers. Through letters, telephone conversations and personal contacts, I've been introduced to so many differences that I've come to believe that no one is *the* right kind of person for youth ministry. But one type makes me cringe. And this type is too great in numbers to ignore.

I recently received a letter from this type of youth worker. He announced that he already had all the knowledge he needed for his work with youth. The wide selection of youth resources available today is "just a review" to him. His recent graduation from college had assured him that he had all the information he needed.

Now, I can believe that "there is nothing new under the sun," but I have a hard time believing that anyone already knows everything under the sun. Especially in youth ministry.

Teenagers constantly change in their reactions to the ever-changing world around them. Even the experts admit that they are not sure if teenagers are normal, or fluctuating psychotics involved in a group manifestation of their disease. Youth sponsors who think they don't need help in their regular involvement with groups of teenagers very likely don't understand teenagers, the world of today or themselves. They very probably have only a superficial image of what's happening around them.

A youth minister who knows everything?

Pity.

Pity the teenagers who must interact with that kind of model of the Christian faith. Pity the people whose problems are pronounced solved by an absolute assumption of knowledge. Pity the kids who face the prospect of hiding their confusions and struggles in order to feel accepted by the all-knowing wonder who blithely pontificates "knowledge" to teenagers.

The one thing I know for sure after nearly 300 semester hours of college and graduate study is that the more you learn, the more you realize how much you don't know.

So, I'm thankful for youth workers who keep searching, growing and learning. I'm proud to share with you in the process of living with God's continuing creation in all its mystery and surprise.

And I'm sure that some have decided all knowledge is in their pocket. I'm angry that some aren't showing youth how to struggle with the processes of discovery. But I'm glad that teenagers have a beautiful ability eventually to see through the presumed serenity of youth workers who think they know everything.

I only hope the delays and detours caused by the "I-know-everything" youth workers are only temporary and not too damaging to the Christian growth of the teenagers around them.

ADDITIONAL READING

The Basic Encyclopedia for Youth Ministry, Dennis C. Benson and Bill Wolfe, Group Books.

Why am I Afraid to Tell You Who I Am?, John Powell, S.J., Argus.

Those rotten, no-good, unexplainable, hard-to-handle, yucky, gloomy, lousy, awful, tiring, imposing, dumb, lingering, debilitating, dismal, frustrating, depressing, rainy-day, distressing, BLAHS.

CHAPTER

40

Say Goodbye To the 'Blahs'

BY JOANI SCHULTZ

The flame is gone. The fire has died. Nothing's really going right. Nothing's really going wrong. You're feeling no real anger or active depression or joy or sadness or fear. No extremes or intensities. No anything. No nothing. In plain and simple terms, you're probably suffering from an acute case of the "blahs."

FEELING THE BLAHS

At some point, everyone experiences that intangible loss of energy and enthusiasm when the zest for creativity dies. Is it possible to overcome the blahs? What can you do with that crazy "can't-quite-put-your-finger-on-it-why" feeling?

Any feeling—be it blah or unblah—needs permission to be felt for awhile. Feelings are not good or bad, right or wrong. Feelings simply *are!* One of the greatest gifts you can give yourself is the freedom to feel what you're feeling. Reserve critical judgments and understand what might be motivating your actions (or lack of them). It's important to recognize, accept and deal with what's going on inside of you.

Yet there are certain feelings that you want to spend as little time with as possible—such as fear, anger, hatred, depression or hurt. The blahs also fall in that get-rid-of-them category.

OVERCOMING THE BLAHS

There are many ways to handle the blahs. The scripture unfolds one perspective for living a life that is "now" and "new." Explore this way of life and watch your blahs fade away.

Be fully in touch with what's going on inside and around you now. Say "goodbye" to existing in the shadow of past failures or successes. Don't let moments slip by while future hopes consume all your energies. Don't play the "what if" game.

The second chapter of Ephesians contains a number of "once you were but *now* you are" statements. Paul's letter expresses the priceless gifts for you in the present. Open yourself to see those gifts of possibilities. God calls you into the full life of today. The living, loving relationship with Jesus is not yesterday's nor tomorrow's. It is yours to be enjoyed—now!

Live the *new*. "Behold, I make all things new" Revelation 21:5). Promise and possibility spring forth from newness. "Your hearts and minds must be made completely new, and you must put on the new self, which is created in God's likeness and reveals itself in the true life that is upright and holy" (Ephesians 4:23-24). Being "new" is a joy you have because of your relationship with Christ.

"New" brings images of birth, beginning, awakening and potential. To celebrate God's creativity, find fresh approaches to living and loving. Absorbing all the newness that surrounds each day can become an incredible adventure.

Learn to live the "now" and "new," and other people will inevitably notice the nice change. How you take care of yourself and your view of life determines how you care for others.

Following are 25 ideas to help you learn to live the "now" and "new." Most days contain the same ingredients—you just need to change the recipe a bit. Transform routine by rearranging one or more of the daily variables. You have unlimited possibilities to creatively blend people, places and things!

25 "BLAHS-AWAY" IDEAS FOR YOU

1. Each morning say a prayer of thanks for God's love and a new day.

2. Tune in a different radio station.

3. Set a "goal of the week."

4. Discover a novel treat that will surprise your taste buds.

5. Buy a fresh flower for yourself (and give it to someone else the next day).

6. If you're usually with people, spend a day alone.

7. If you're usually alone, spend a day with people.

8. Learn to say "I love you" in a different language.

9. Listen to silence; make it into a melody.

10. Choose a "word of the week"—speak it, write it, sing it, color it and juggle it.

11. Declare the day National Chocolate Day/Purple Day/ Daisy Day/Hug Day/ or "Twos" Day.

12. Whisper instead of shouting or talking in a normal voice.

13. Sip and savor a specialty coffee or herbal tea.

14. Order something different on a menu.

15. Light a scented candle and say a prayer of gratitude for someone who's been a light in your life.

16. Window-shop.

17. Look for faith and truth object lessons in the world around you and write your insights in a journal.

18. Rearrange the furniture in your room or office.

19. Walk somewhere you usually drive.

20. Select a scripture verse for the day—memorize it, sing it, paint it, make it yours.

21. Create a unique signature that expresses the real you.

22. Start a collection of anything.

23. Each week send a surprise note to a long-lost, ever-present or newly found friend. Express your thankfulness to God for the friend.

24. Record conversations, sounds or music on a cassette tape and send it to a special friend or family member.

25. Send someone you know their very own "Beat the

Blahs" kit—complete with confetti, balloons, streamers and a stick of gum.

ADDITIONAL READING

Feelings, Willard Gaylin, Harper and Row.

Living, Loving and Learning, Leo Buscaglia, Holt, Rinehart and Winston.

Everyone has fallen down
or not lived up to expectations. It's how we react
that's important.

Failure— What to Do If You Stumble

BY LARRY KEEFAUVER

All of us have stumbled at one time or another. And we've all felt the pain of failure. We haven't lived up to the expectations of our young people, peers or superiors. Or, maybe we've simply blown it.

Even worse than most of our failures is the fear that we're going to fail. The less we reach out and make ourselves vulnerable, the fewer chances we have to fail. If we don't start something risky, there's no chance we may not finish it. Or maybe we've actually stumbled and experienced the pain of failure before.

Whatever your failure, whether it affects your entire group or just you personally, it can be a source of tremendous personal and spiritual growth.

So, how do we create a climate that minimizes the fear of failure or lets us deal with the pain when we do stumble and fall?

I'd like to offer three suggestions:
- Understand ourselves and our fear of failure
- Learn from failure

● Program for success

UNDERSTAND OURSELVES AND OUR FEARS

A Gallup poll revealed that only 35 percent of Protestants and 39 percent of Catholics possess strong self-esteem. Low self-esteem infects not only youth but also adults who work with them. Low self-esteem contributes to our fear of failure—both for ourselves and the youth with whom we work. Our low self-esteem also makes it difficult for us to build strong self-worth in those youth in our groups.

Intertwined with our low self-esteem are irrational beliefs and attitudes that are rooted in unrealistic expectations of ourselves and others. Some of the irrational beliefs we are particularly susceptible to as youth workers are:

I need the love and approval of every significant person in my life. We want everyone in the church and youth group to love us and approve of what we do. Yet, trying to please everyone all the time is impossible. In trying to be all things to all people, we doom ourselves to failure. The bottom line shouldn't be to please everyone else. Rather, it should be to please God. We think success is measured by great numbers coming to youth meetings; dozens of youth becoming Christians; exciting programs that kids stand in line for; and glowing praise from pastor, church leaders and youth alike.

A seminary professor helped me shatter this irrational way of thinking when he said, "God doesn't require us to be successful, but faithful." When we try to please God, our priorities are correct and fears of failure are diminished. The fact that we can do all things through Christ who strengthens us also gives us added strength to face failure.

I must be competent and adequate in everything related to youth ministry. Often I've not tried youth events because I feared my lack of knowledge or expertise would spell failure. We do not have to know everything. However, we do need a desire to learn and an eagerness to share ourselves—both weaknesses and strengths. Some of the times of greatest success for me in youth ministry have come when I've risked failure and shared my feelings of anxiety and inadequacy with the youth. When I admitted I didn't know it all, they reached out to me in support and care.

People who fail deserve to be blamed. This irrational belief leads us to be too hard on ourselves and our youth in the midst of failure. Condemning others when they fail destroys any support we may need in the future when we fail.

The Apostle Paul gives us a corrective for this irrational belief: "We who are strong ought to bear with the failings of the weak and not to please ourselves. Each of us should please his neighbor for his good, to build him up" (Romans 15:1-2).

I can't settle for less than the perfect solution to my problem. Working in relationship with others in a youth group (adults, parents or the youth) involves compromise. Compromise doesn't have to involve the altering of our essential beliefs, doctrines or values. Often compromise comes when we plan events and have to arrive at the best strategy and direction. Our solutions are not always the best for a situation.

Bring others into your decision-making process so that if failure occurs, all can share in working through the problem and in supporting one another. If plans are successful, all can rejoice. Our desires for perfectionism directly contribute to failure or inability to work effectively with others.

LEARN FROM FAILURE

When expectations of ourselves or others are not met and we feel a sense of failure, ask:
- Is this my problem or someone else's?
- Are my expectations for myself and others in youth ministry unrealistic?
- What have I learned from this?
- Can I believe that although I have failed at one thing, I am not a failure?

One failure doesn't make us a failure. I have seen so many adults give up on youth ministry on the basis of one unpleasant experience, one failure. That is tragic. We need positive attitudes. Certainly we will make mistakes. We will fail from time to time. But the possibility of building Christian relationships and faith with youth far outweighs any possibility of failure.

Let us remember that our response to failure is often as important as what has actually happened. We can respond positively and seek a constructive solution or we can blame ourselves and others.

When we fail and are responsible, we need to go to the

people who are affected by the failures and seek forgiveness and a renewed relationship.

Here are actions to take when you fail:

1. Take responsibility that is genuinely yours.

2. Ask for forgiveness. Instead of simply saying, "I'm sorry," say, "I need you to forgive me. Will you?"

3. Make amends. Take positive steps toward restitution in the present and make plans to avoid future mistakes.

4. Move on. Put the guilt behind you. Don't let past failures rob you of present effectiveness.

PROGRAM FOR SUCCESS

How can you reduce the possibilities of failure? There are six basic directions in youth ministry you can take to encourage success and cope with failure.

1. Develop a support group. Youth and youth workers should try to meet together on a regular basis for planning, evaluating, praying and encouraging one another.

2. Communicate. Failure often results from poor communication. Communicate with everyone who needs to know: not only the youth, but also other youth workers, parents, church leaders and the pastor. You can't over communicate.

3. Remember the little things. Make checklists. I once went on an overnight lock-in where one of the adults working forgot the meat for the hamburgers. The adult purchasing the food tried to remember everything without writing anything down.

4. Laugh with each other. Don't take yourself too seriously. A youth group with a sense of humor can cope with failure much more effectively than ever-serious, always-somber groups.

5. Program to meet the needs of youth. Much of failure in youth ministry happens when either the church or the youth workers program to meet their own needs. When we focus on the whole person—the spiritual, physical, emotional and intellectual needs of youth—then we can plan successful programs. Assess their needs. Program to meet those needs.

6. Plan ahead. No matter how much happens at the last minute, we risk failure by starting too late. Procrastination often spells failure and doom for retreats, trips and the evening fellowship. Plan in advance.

ARE YOU TOO MUCH OF A PERFECTIONIST?

Take this quiz to help you evaluate your need for success and perfection. Rate yourself 1 to 5 using this scale:

+ 2 for strongly agreeing with a statement
+ 1 for agreeing
0 for feeling neutral or undecided
− 1 for disagreeing
− 2 for strongly disagreeing

____ 1. I should be angry with the youth or myself if something goes wrong.

____ 2. The youth will think less of me if I fail.

____ 3. If I or the youth don't set the highest standards for ourselves and the group, we'll end up as a second-rate group.

____ 4. We shouldn't make the same mistake twice.

____ 5. I would feel bad for failing to live up to my expectations or the youths'.

____ 6. If I'm really tough on myself or others when there is failure, that toughness will help eliminate failure in the future.

____ 7. If I try hard enough, anything I tackle will be a success.

____ 8. If we can't do something well in youth ministry, then we shouldn't try it at all.

____ 9. It is a poor Christian model for me to show weakness, admit uncertainty or let the youth group see me fail at a task.

____ 10. Anything that seems average is bound to be unsatisfying to me or the youth.

Now add up your total. The highest degree of perfectionism is + 20. The lowest is − 20. The closer your score is to + 20, the more the fear of failure influences and paralyzes your ability to work with youth. Each of us has high expectations of ourselves and others. But when those expectations demand that we or others be perfect, we set ourselves up for failure.

A PERSONAL NOTE TO YOU

You may be hurting right now because of a failure in the past. That hurt probably is producing a fear of failure in the future. I encourage you to do something now about the pain in order to conquer the fear of failure. Sit down and talk with a trusted Christian friend. Pray for God's healing and guidance. Find a support group with peers, pastor or other Christians who will encourage you in youth ministry.

Don't try to go it alone. We are one body in Jesus Christ. When one hurts, we all hurt. When one rejoices, we all rejoice. In youth ministry, youth and adults work together to bear our weakness and celebrate our strengths.

ADDITIONAL READING

The God of the Second Chance, Dean Merrill, Zondervan.
Letting Go: Uncomplicating Your Life, Ramona S. Adams, Herbert A. Otto and Audeane S. Cowley, Macmillan.

A whirlwind of ministry
activities can leave you
drained. Yet, you must
keep your faith alive and
growing.

CHAPTER
42

Putting the Light Back Into Your Life

BY JOANI SCHULTZ

Have you ever found yourself being whipped around by a whirlwind of ministry activities? Has your schedule swept you into collapse or exhaustion? There's no question that heavy involvement in youth ministry can lead to personal and spiritual weariness. A schedule laden with youth meetings, activities, lock-ins, retreats, preparation and planning chips away at the boundary that separates your job with how you feel about yourself.

Keeping that spiritual light alive in your life is one of the great ministry challenges. Balancing the teeter-totter between giving to others and receiving for yourself is a process that never stops.

LIFE IN ALL ITS FULLNESS

Jesus said, "I have come in order that you might have life—life in all its fullness" (John 10:10b). Fullness?

"That's just great," you say. "My days are so hectic and every moment is so packed, I'm like a pressurized can ready to explode. I don't need any more fullness. Help!"

But Jesus had a different kind of "fullness" in mind. The fullness in your life must be more than a rapid pace and a marathon schedule. Somewhere in the whirlwind of busyness, you must consciously keep your perspective of life in focus.

Here's one view of living that can help make growth and newness a daily occurrence. Are you ready? Stop and take a deep breath.

VIEW YOUR LIFE AS A WINDOW

Try this experiment. Imagine your life and ministry as a window. What happens if you look only at the glass instead of through it to the world beyond? You will see smudges and specks. There might even be a forgotten streak from the last cleaning job.

Your life may be like that windowpane. Instead of looking through it to see what's on the outside, you will be distracted by the smears.

Those smudges and specks can block out the spiritual light if you let them get in the way. Before long you forget the fullness God intends for your life.

Don't get me wrong. Looking beyond and through circumstances doesn't mean avoiding or not dealing with them. It simply means keeping a positive perspective, always looking for growth; it's watching for the good things, the God-things in life.

Being involved in youth ministry is not without its unsightly streaks and smudges. Let's take a look at a few of those hard-to-handle situations. Check and see how you usually respond.

TAKE THIS WINDOWPANE TEST

Situation one: There's a lack of parental support in your youth ministry program. It really showed up when you advertised the annual Summertime Big Trip. Instead of understanding the growth and value of the trip, parents questioned the reasoning for the event. Many of them even discouraged their teenagers' participation.

What do you do?

● Growl and complain that no one ever understands you.

● Think of canceling the trip; in fact, the idea of going fishing instead sounds rather appealing.

● Use this as an excellent opportunity to communicate a healthy and wholistic view of youth ministry.

Situation two: You discover Todd has been smoking pot on the youth retreat.

What do you do?

● Clench your teeth (and fists) in anger.

● Throw up your hands in despair.

● Face the challenge. See this as a perfect opening for caring and honest confrontation between Todd and you.

Situation three: You look back at your calendar and realize the last time you took an honest-to-goodness day off was three months ago.

What do you do?

● Destroy your calendar so you won't be reminded.

●·Wallow awhile in self-pity.

● Take initiative to treat yourself and set a goal for taking personal time *at least* once a week.

If you chose the last answer to each situation as your usual response—congratulations! You've begun the challenge of viewing life transparently.

YOUR FAITH-LIFE

The windowpane view of life is one way of acknowledging that *all* life is wrapped in faith. Living by faith means seeing situations transparently. It is in looking beyond and seeing through that you become actively involved in the growth process. You're ready to face challenges and become all you can be in ministry.

When you do this, faith becomes much more than trusting in the gift of life after death. It's trusting the full life you have *now* because you're connected with Christ. The call to stay close and spend time on your God-relationship remains. God continuously turns old to new, sickness to health, death to life and defeat to victory.

As you begin to look at life this way, remember: You are not in this alone. Your struggles are shared with a God who knows struggle—your victories are shared with a God who brings victory! You're invited to live energized and empowered by God's spirit. Ephesians rings with words of strength: "And how very great is his power at work in us who believe. This power working in us is the same mighty strength which he used when he raised Christ from death

and seated him at his right side in the heavenly world"
(Ephesians 1:19-20).

IDEAS FOR SPIRITUAL GROWTH

Whether you need a gentle nudge or forceful shove to take
action on your own personal growth—do it! Choose from one
or more of these nudges or shoves. You know best which
method will bring peace and new life to you.

Get involved with the Bible. God's spirit gets into you as
you get into the Word. Jesus reminded us, "If you remain in
me and my words in you, then you will ask for anything you
wish, and you shall have it" (John 15:7). Discipline yourself
to read portions of scripture daily. A simple resource for
structuring daily Bible reading can be ordered from the
American Bible Society, 1865 Broadway, New York, NY
10023. For pennies you can buy a Bible reading guide. You
might even want to order one for a friend.

Browse through a Christian bookstore. There's a banquet
of devotional possibilities awaiting you. Choose a Bible study
guide for your personal use.

Make an effort to be a part of a Bible class—one that
you're not leading.

Establish a day off. Set a certain day of the week as your
day. Inform the congregational members of the importance,
the sacredness, of that time. Even God took a day off! If you
need to be reminded of that, read Genesis 2:3. "He blessed
the seventh day and set it apart as a special day because by
that day he had completed his creation and stopped working." If God saw the importance of time off, you can too.

Do something that gets tangible results. Seeing actual,
tangible, touchable results in "people work" is rare. To reward you with a sense of accomplishment, find an activity
or hobby that gives an actual, seeable outcome. Odd as it
seems, I developed a love for housecleaning, just because I
could see what I had accomplished.

Read a book. Your book selection can be faith-related, but
feel free to absorb yourself in a book for sheer entertainment. By reading something that's not work-related, you can
spark new avenues of creativity and energy.

Find a support person. Galatians 6:2 says, "Help carry
one another's burdens, and in this way you will obey the
law of Christ." In sharing mutual woes and wows you

energize each other. What a privilege it is to be God's instrument and bring strength and support to someone.

Listen to cassette tapes. Many people spend a lot of time in the car. Listening provides creative use of on-the-road time. Listen to Christian music, special speakers or last Sunday's sermon. Or why not use the tape to record your own thoughts and feelings? Play back your reflections and listen to yourself. See what you discover from your own words by staying in touch with what's going on inside of you.

ADDITIONAL READING

Celebration of Discipline, Richard J. Foster, Harper and Row.

The Christian's Diary: A Personal Journal for Bible Study, Prayer, and Spiritual Growth, Frances Loftiss Carroll, Prentice-Hall.

You are a busy person. You care about young people, but have just two hours a week to give. What can you do?

CHAPTER
43

Help! Only Two Hours For Youth Work

BY J. DAVID STONE

O nly two hours a week to do youth ministry . . . .
I've been there. I know what it's like to care deeply about young people but not have much time to do anything about it.

I've felt the adrenalin squirt through my system as I've started a youth group meeting not knowing what I was going to do in the next five minutes.

It's not a good feeling, and it's not good for the youth group either.

What do you do when you have only a couple of hours a week to do youth ministry? Where do you start? How can you best use your time?

GET THE MOST FROM TWO HOURS A WEEK

The most pronounced need young people have today is for a stronger self-image, and self-image develops through having positive relationships. Young people grow spiritually when they receive spiritual guidance from loving, caring adults.

All that takes times.

To be the best steward of your time, I suggest that you break your time into three categories: personal visitation, program planning and the actual program. Give personal visitation the biggest chunk of your time—an hour. The other two categories warrant 30 minutes each. This time management allows for at least 75 percent of your youth ministry efforts to be spent *with* youth: 50 percent through visitation and 25 percent through the program time.

PERSONAL VISITATION

Visit one-on-one with your young people in their homes. This may take a while, but it's worth the effort. You'll get to know individual group members better, and they'll never forget that you cared enough to spend time with them.

Visit your young people in their social settings. You might do this every other week. Meet with several of them during their lunch period at school; attend part or all of a school function, such as a talent show or basketball game, in which some of your group members are involved. By being on their turf, you'll establish positive bonding with your young people. You'll better understand what's important to them and what influences their lives outside of church.

PROGRAM PLANNING

Assign portions of the program to the youth themselves and have weekly or semimonthly meetings of a half hour or hour to check on assignments and talk through the leadership process. In other words, let the youth help you prepare the program.

Follow up carefully with everyone who has responsibilities to see that everything is in order before the meetings. Group members who have done their assignments will gladly come to your home for punch and cookies.

Some youth workers with limited time share the responsibilities—schedules are set up so that the youth workers trade off the program planning duties. If you are participating in such a program, then you will have weeks with 30 minutes of "free time" when the planning is not your responsibility. If so, great! Use that time to be with your young people.

THE PROGRAM

Arrive a few minutes early. Be the first person to greet the newcomers or regular attenders.

If you're leading the program, look for opportunities to comment on good responses or positive behavior of group members. A simple "What a neat thought" or "I like the way you role played that hard situation" can mean a lot to young people who are struggling with a weak self-image. Such remarks also may encourage shy group members to become more involved in the meetings.

If you are an adviser or counselor for the meeting, sit with the group members. Take advantage of every opportunity to get to know them better. Risk yourself; initiate a conversation and establish common ground. Talk about music, sports, hobbies or vacations. Use the moments before and after the program to develop positive relationships with the young people.

A CHALLENGE

I have observed that people gravitate toward the things they enjoy and with which they feel comfortable.

I also have noticed that as adults get to know young people and spend more time with them, their uneasiness disappears and they find they really do enjoy and feel comfortable with the youth.

If you have only two hours a week for youth ministry, spend at least 75 percent of it developing relationships with your young people. You will discover you have more time than you realized.

BUILD RELATIONSHIPS WITH YOUR YOUTH

If you plan to spend 75 percent of your time *with* the young people, where do you go? What do you do? Where do you begin? Use these ideas as a springboard to building relationships. It can be the beginning of exciting and special friendships with you and your young people.

Time on Their Turf

● Visit the teenagers in their homes. Set an appointment two weeks in advance. Remind them of your plans a few days before your visit. When you go, spend the time getting to know who they are. Follow up your visit with a phone call. Keep a card file which includes special dates, hobbies, interests and other useful information for your youth ministry efforts.

● Eat lunch with them in their school cafeteria. Ask one person to meet you at lunchtime. Have him or her escort you to the cafeteria. Enjoy talking with your youth group members and their school friends.

● Attend extracurricular activities in which the young people are involved. Be aware of dates for football, basketball and soccer games; gym and swimming meets; music concerts and plays; or pep squad practices. Find out the schedules. If you are unable to attend an entire event, drop by for a short while. This expresses that you share their interests.

Shared Activity Time

● Think of an activity or interest you could share with a young person. Fun one-on-one ideas include baking cookies, making caramel corn, practicing guitar, sharing a hobby, learning a new skill together, waxing or fixing a car, or walking in the park.

● Share a food time together. Meet someone for breakfast before school one day or treat yourselves to an ice cream cone or soda pop after school. Eating together provides an opportunity for conversation and growth of friendship.

● Invite a young person to join you as you run errands. If you've got a few things to do and it involves driving a distance, ask a young person to accompany you—just to talk. Riding in a car allows precious time to talk, you accomplish your errands and you build a friendship.

Time, like every other
resource, can be well-used
or wasted. How effectively
do you manage your
ministry?

CHAPTER

44

Managing Your Time in Youth Ministry

"**D**ost thou love life? Then do not squander time, for that is the stuff life is made of."—Ben Franklin

"The management of time should be the No. 1 priority for us. Without some organization of your day, it will waste away without purpose and drain away without accomplishment."—C. Neil Strait

"A slothful man will not catch his prey . . ."—Proverbs 12:27.

A young minister recently suffered a heart attack. At 33, his heart finally gave up trying to compensate for what his physician said was ultimately a poor use of time. Too many meetings, visits, office tasks, sermons. Too little exercise, good food, leisure and planning of time.

Time is neither friend nor foe. Like every resource, it can be well-used or wasted. IBM management consultant Bob Haughey offers these helpful, time-efficient tools:

THE TASK FILE

Tired of the cluttered desk? A task file can help you get

organized. You need 12 letter-size (11¾ x 9½) manila file folders, 31 file dividers and one or two hanging folders.

Label the file folders January through December. Number the dividers one through 31—one for each day of the month. Place the file folders in a hanging file, the days of the current month first, then the coming 11 months.

As tasks come up, place them in the appropriate file folder. Put notes, memos, reminders, letters, etc., in the file folders according to a realistic plan for completing the tasks. Update the folders monthly moving the upcoming months' tasks forward and rotating the just completed month's file to the back.

For example, at the first of the year, separate January's folder into 31 days. Place the other months in sequence to December.

The task file takes a few minutes each day to maintain. However, you'll find this time among the best spent of the day. Simply keeping track of the days', weeks', and months' tasks provides a stable framework for getting things done.

THE TIME QUIZ

If you want an idea of how effectively you manage your time, give yourself the following quiz:

1. Do I have in writing a clearly defined set of long-range goals?

2. Do I have a similar set of goals for the next six months?

3. Do I have something each day to move me closer to my goals?

4. Do I have a written list of what I want to accomplish at work every day?

5. Do I try to do the most important tasks during my prime time (when I am most fresh and energetic)?

6. Do I concentrate on accomplishment instead of activity?

7. Do I set priorities according to importance, not urgency?

8. Do I make constructive use of travel time?

9. Have I taken steps to prevent unneeded information and publications from reaching my desk and intruding on my time?

10. Do I try to put work out of my mind when away from

the office, except in clear emergencies?

11. Do I force myself to make minor decisions quickly?

12. Am I on guard against a recurring crisis, taking steps to make sure that it won't occur again?

13. Do I force myself to take time to plan?

14. Do I make periodic use of a time log to determine whether I am slipping back into unproductive routines?

15. Am I continually striving to establish habits that will make me more effective?

16. Do I keep in mind the dollar value of my time?

17. Am I always late for meetings?

18. Do I routinely feel I accomplish very little of what I wanted to do?

19. Do I have several tasks at work (or home) which I want to do but have not found the time?

20. Do I always answer the telephone no matter what I am doing?

THE TIME LOG

Another helpful tool for analyzing and improving your time management is the time log. This tool looks at the day-to-day use of time.

First, make several copies of the following hour-by-hour time log:

How I Spent My Time

6 a.m.	
7 a.m.	
8 a.m.	
9 a.m.	
10 a.m.	
11 a.m.	
Noon	
1 p.m.	
2 p.m.	
3 p.m.	
4 p.m.	
5 p.m.	
6 p.m.	
7 p.m.	

8 p.m.	
9 p.m.	
10 p.m.	
11 p.m.	

After you have completed a time log for several days, evaluate the entries carefully and ask yourself:

1. What am I doing that does not really have to be done?
2. What am I doing that could be done by someone else?
3. What am I doing that could be done more efficiently?
4. What am I doing that wastes the time of others?

Save your daily "to do" lists for several days. Analyze the lists by asking the following questions:

1. Were my lists really adequate? Or were my lists mainly an accumulation of the tasks which happened to force themselves on my attention?
2. Did I mark the two or three items each day which would be considered the "critical few"? Did I schedule a block of time to take care of each of these high-priority items?
3. What are the recurring low-priority tasks which I should try to schedule during low-energy times?

Keep a list of interruptions, both phone and personal. Then ask yourself:

1. Who or what is responsible for most of my interruptions?
2. Am I getting calls that really should go to someone else? What can I do about this?
3. Have I set aside a period of time in the morning and in the afternoon as quiet time to be spent in concentrated effort on major tasks?
4. Do I force people to interrupt me with questions by failing to keep them fully informed so that they must repeatedly ask for additional information?
5. Could regularly scheduled availability times or meetings eliminate some of the interruptions?

ADDITIONAL READING

Getting a Grip on Time Management, Les Christie, Victor.
How to Stop Procrastinating and Start Living, Loren Broadus, Augsburg.

The best-made programs
cover three important
elements: people, resources
and preparation.

CHAPTER 45

How to Plan For Success

BY ROGER DILL

It started out as a pleasant lunch and a nice break from the office. But the conversation quickly moved toward issues facing my lunch partner Ralph, a youth pastor at a neighboring church. "Certain members of the church council are getting down on me for low attendance at the youth group," he said candidly.

"Low attendance," I thought to myself. "The old numbers game."

Our conversation continued for another hour and a half as Ralph expressed his frustration, hurt and confusion. The council wanted to see "results" in terms of numbers of kids.

After he had voiced his frustration, I asked him, "So, Ralph, what's your plan?" His face went blank. I couldn't tell whether I had said a taboo word or if he really didn't have a plan. The latter was the case.

Ralph is not much different from a number of us. Most of us believe in setting goals and laying out plans (sometimes for up to three years). But fewer of us turn those plans into successful events, studies and activities.

One of the greatest dangers in the planning process is the tendency to forget three important elements.

IMPORTANT ELEMENT NO. 1: PEOPLE

This sounds, of course, like an oversimplification. After all, who could conduct a youth ministry without youth? But young people often get neglected in the planning process.

Ask yourself, "How much do I know about the members of my group?" Certainly you know some better than others. You know the group's needs better if this is your third year with them rather than your first. In planning your schedule for the next few months, what needs will you concentrate on meeting?

One year after beginning my job as youth director, I sat down and asked myself the following questions:

1. How many young people are presently involved in the group?

2. How long have most of them been involved?

3. How many guys are involved? girls?

4. What's my relationship with the guys? girls?

5. What are the three biggest needs of the group as I perceive them now?

6. Are there unhealthy cliques in the group? in the staff?

7. How many volunteer staff are returning from last year? are more needed?

8. What three activities/camps have been most successful in the past?

9. What regular meetings will I plan and how will they compare with last year's meetings?

10. How many schools are within a 15-mile radius of the church facility? List them.

After answering each of the questions, I decided to go one step further and ask the group. Because it was my first year with the new group, I was at a disadvantage. But the Student Survey on page 230 helped tremendously.

The Student Survey is important because it communicates to the young people that their opinions matter to you. The survey is another way of telling them that they own the ministry.

As you make specific plans, remember that programs are designed to fit your youth, not vice versa. A well-designed program will:

● **Stretch them mentally.** Today's youth are able to digest challenging and stimulating materials, concepts and principles. It is a sin to bore them with shallow and carelessly planned meetings.

● **Challenge them spiritually.** Most youth respond positively to a challenge. Help them set a particular goal (i.e., memorize three verses a week, have a 15-minute devotion each day, talk to one friend about Christ). Then support them in reaching that goal.

● **Provide physical expression.** In the course of leading a small group of freshman guys, I found it helpful to play basketball before studying together. There is a need to release energy. There is also a need for proper expression of care through a slap on the back, a handshake or a hug of encouragement.

● **Offer social interaction.** Friendships can be hard to come by, but are absolutely needed in the youth years. A balanced program should try to help the kids get closer to each other.

IMPORTANT ELEMENT NO. 2: RESOURCES

Determine what resources you have available in three areas: people, facilities and equipment.

● **Utilize volunteers.** Many youth leaders try to do the entire youth ministry by themselves. This approach leads to mental and spiritual burnout—even the martyr syndrome: "I am the only person who can run this program effectively."

After 10 years of being involved in different types of youth ministry, I believe that volunteers are the most valuable resource in youth ministry.

But be careful! Don't just give volunteers menial tasks to perform. They can do much more than collect name cards, pass out pencils or serve refreshments. You can build a sense of ownership by giving volunteers such significant responsibilities as leading a small group, teaching a Bible study, leading music, counseling at camp or having weekly appointments with students.

● **Consider the facility.** The atmosphere a meeting place sets either greatly adds to or detracts from the purpose of the meeting. If your group is small, don't meet in a 300-seat auditorium. If your meeting is designed to reach non-Christians, a neutral site like a recreation room or clubhouse is sometimes better than meeting at the church.

● **Evaluate equipment.** The following form should help you evaluate equipment needs within your own group.

Equipment Item	Needed	Not Needed	Approx. Cost	Date Needed
Video cassette recorder	☐	☐	$ _____	_____
16 mm projector	☐	☐	$ _____	_____
8 mm projector (with sound)	☐	☐	$ _____	_____
P.A. system (portable)	☐	☐	$ _____	_____
Cassette deck	☐	☐	$ _____	_____
Overhead projector	☐	☐	$ _____	_____
Overhead transparencies	☐	☐	$ _____	_____
Screen	☐	☐	$ _____	_____
Blackboard (pref. portable)	☐	☐	$ _____	_____
Extra Bibles	☐	☐	$ _____	_____
Small group manuals	☐	☐	$ _____	_____
Special handouts/pencils	☐	☐	$ _____	_____
Drama/skit props	☐	☐	$ _____	_____
Recreation/sports equipment	☐	☐	$ _____	_____

STUDENT SURVEY

A. ☐ Male
   ☐ Female
   ☐ Freshman
   ☐ Sophomore
   ☐ Junior
   ☐ Senior
   How long have you been involved in the youth program?
   ☐ 0-3 months
   ☐ 3-6 months
   ☐ 6 months/1 year
   ☐ 1-2 years
   ☐ over 2 years

B. 1. Would you like to join a small group? ☐Yes ☐No
   2. The one thing I like best about our group is
   _____

3. The one thing I dislike most about our group is
   _____

4. If you could change two things about this group, what would they be?
   _____

5. The three best activities/camps that I have been to are:
   1._____
   2._____
   3._____

C. Complete the following sentences:
   1. God is _____
   2. The Bible is _____
   3. My family is _____
   4. My looks are _____

IMPORTANT ELEMENT NO. 3: PREPARATION

You'll probably have times in your ministry when the most creative plans will be defeated by trying to do too much in too little time. So, when planning your programs consider these basics first:

Sunday Morning
Purpose: Growth
Elements: Group singing, group sharing/prayer, expository teaching
Length: 1 hour 15 minutes

Midweek Meeting
Purpose: Outreach
Elements: Group singing, games (optional), live music, media, drama, message (15 to 20 minutes)
Length: 1 hour 30 minutes
Facility: High school auditorium

---

5. My favorite sport/hobby is _____

6. My favorite music group is _____

7. My favorite movie is

_____

8. A Christian is_____

_____

D. 1. If you could study any book in the Bible, what would you study and why?

_____

2. If you could explore five of the following topics, which would you choose (circle five)?

- loneliness
- family
- anger
- guilt/ forgiveness
- fear
- peer pressure
- prayer
- church
- self-esteem
- commitment
- friendship
- prejudice
- love
- sex/dating
- verbal cruelty
- happiness
- other _____

- heaven
- drinking/ drugs
- death/ suicide
- Jesus
- marriage
- depres- sion
- God
- honesty
- quiet time
- parents
- future
- resur- rection
- music
- failure/ success

Small Groups
   Purpose: Discipleship
   Elements: Group sharing/prayer, study
   Length: Varies (usually 1 to 2 hours)
   Meetings: Weekly
   Facility: Varies (homes, offices, restaurants, park, etc.)

Staff Meetings
   Purpose: Planning/training
   Elements: Teaching, prayer, planning sessions
   Length: Varies (1 to 2 hours)
   Meetings: Once/twice monthly

Fall Kickoff Meeting (Early September)
   Possible activities include:
   ● Concert with Christian group (either local or profes-
     sional).
   ● Leadership breakfast (to reunite last year's stu-
     dent leaders to plan and pray together).
   ● Freshman swim party (includes special invitations, pool
     games, student speakers, etc. Gives incoming students
     an opportunity to hear about the group).

Halloween
   ● Costume party with special movie or music group and
     speaker dealing with the theme of "fear."
   ● Going to local "haunted house" and meeting together
     afterward.
   ● Your group takes a local orphanage "trick or treating"
     and provides a party for the kids afterward.

Thanksgiving
   ● Food drive for the needy.
   ● "Let It Growl Night," featuring a one-day fast with a
     special time of prayer and sharing in the evening.
   ● A special night of programming based on the theme:
     "Giving Thanks to God."

Christmas:
   Although meeting on Christmas is not feasible, it is possi-
ble to plan one or more of the following before or just after
Christmas:
   ● Sponsor a family in the area, providing them with food
     and gifts for Christmas.
   ● Youth night at church with the group performing its

version of Dickens' **A Christmas Carol.**
- Progressive dinner and Christmas story. With each portion of the meal, another part of the Christmas story is read or enacted.
- To emphasize the theme of giving, have your youth group sponsor a Christmas party for a local orphanage, juvenile hall or convalescent hospital.

New Year's Eve
- All night party at a bowling alley.
- All night party including movies, ice cream or roller skating, and a serious time of worship (perhaps candle ceremony).
- Plan a three-day retreat to bring in the New Year.

Weekend Retreat
The facilities available, the climate of a particular area and the purpose of the retreat will dictate when and how many retreats/conferences to have. Following are possible options:
- Fall leadership/planning retreat with student advisory council and volunteers.
- Staff planning/training retreat.
- Winter camp (keep in mind travel time, cost, weather, i.e., possibility of no snow).
- Small group retreats (organized and conducted by each individual small group).

All the above meetings, activities and camps have one central purpose: offering a balanced experience with the goal of spiritual and personal growth.

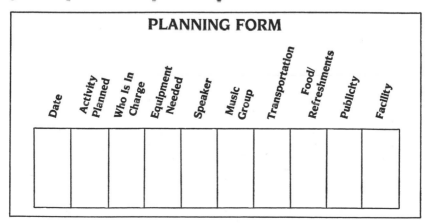

PLANNING FORM

Date	Activity Planned	Who Is In Charge	Equipment Needed	Speaker	Music Group	Transportation	Food/ Refreshments	Publicity	Facility

How far ahead should you plan for activities? I suggest preparing a plan for at least the upcoming four months. If you can accomplish that goal, then attempt a three-year master plan. The Planning Form on page 233 can help you get started. Your plan should be firm enough to direct the program, yet flexible in order to meet the needs of your youth.

Planning is not a dirty word. You need not get caught in the same trap as my friend Ralph. The more you plan, the more you will succeed in your youth ministry.

Keeping Up-to-Date With Kids

Is it Jay who plays basketball— or is it football? Is it Karen or Chris who can't meet on Wednesday nights because of guitar lessons?

When you're dealing with lots of kids, simple details are difficult to keep organized in your head. Use this tried-and-true file card idea.

● Start by asking your kids to write basic information about themselves on 3 × 5 cards.

> name   grade
> favorite school subject
> extracurricular activities
> hobbies
> foreign language, if taking one

● Maintain your file cards by jotting notes on them as your young people keep you informed about their lives (such as seasonal sports activities, lead in the school play).

● Keep your file cards near the phone. When Sue calls, you can refer to her card and remember to ask her how her volleyball team is doing. Using the cards to jog your memory will help your kids feel you really care about them.

● Creatively use your file cards. If you hear Tim is having trouble with algebra, check to see which group member listed algebra as his or her favorite subject. You could make a match they'll thank you for.

—Cindy Parolini

ADDITIONAL READING

The Art of Management for Christian Leaders, Ted Engstrom, Word.

Getting Organized, Stephanie Winston, Warner.

Managing Your Time, Ted Engstrom and Alex MacKenzie, Zondervan.

Caring for and ministering
with youth is one of the
greatest pressure-building
occupations around. Learn
how to control stressful
events in your life.

CHAPTER
46

Take Control
Of the Stress
In Your Life

BY BILL STEARNS

Whenever my stomach was in knots, I'd visualize the
headline: "Hapless Local Youth Leader Found
Dead!" The subhead would be: "Demanding Ministries
Suspected."

You well know the pain of being stretched in two different
directions (or four or 16) by the pressures of typical youth
work. Youth ministry is filled with stress; nobody said it
would be easy.

STRESS IS EASY TO GET

Saying "yes" to youth ministry can be the first step in the
process toward a stressful life. A simple assent to working
with youth instantly presents you with pressures from kids,
their parents, your church or organization, God, your own
children or family, your spouse, your closest friend or
yourself. Stress comes with the territory. But it isn't all bad.
Stressors—factors bringing pressures on you—can be negative: Your ski retreat bus blows a second tire 40 miles from
nowhere at 3 a.m. Or, stress can be positive: You're pro-

moted to a more desired position in the youth program.

The way you handle positive or negative stress can set the pace for your ministry. Stress can bring the exultation of "a strong man running a race" (Psalm 19:5). But when stress is handled poorly, it becomes distress.

YOU AND DISTRESS

First, recognize the danger: As a youth worker, you prob-

WHERE DOES STRESS COME FROM?

Stress squeezes you on all fronts. Here are some of the typical stressors I have confronted in youth ministry:

● My wife pleaded that I stay home instead of supervising recreation:

She: There's got to be somebody else who can do it.

Me: I tried 'em all. I have to go.

Regarding the later deacon's meeting:

She: Do you *have* to go to those all the time?

Me: It's in my job description.

● My supervising pastor insisted I be back in the office the morning after returning from a strenuous two-week missions trip, and I thought to myself, "Is everybody in real adult life this tired all the time?"

● The business administrator looked at us church staff members and asked, "Since the building program is under way and new members are needed to foot the bill, is each of you bringing in enough people to justify your being here?"

These situations are actually forms of expectations, and expectations bring stress. People will expect you to worship the Old World Work Ethic ("Sunday is a day of rest, so it's considered as your day off like every other working stiff"), and to cherish the Martyrdom of Ministry ("ministers are supposed to be poor").

The board members will expect you to _____.

Your family or spouse expects you to _____.

Your youth expect _____.

They expect certain things from you, which puts stress on you. Stress becomes distress when you feel you can't do anything about the ways their expectations don't match. If you aren't accomplishing what you think you ought to be, if your supervisors expect more from you than you can possibly put out, if your youth want you to pull off dazzling activities every time, if your family or friends demand more time than you can give, if your youths' parents ask for more emotional energy than you can cough up, and—watch the wording—if *you think* God requires more commitment from you than you can give, you're distressed.

ably are a notorious achiever (dynamic, goal-oriented idealist) and comer (aspiring climber using youth work as a stepping stone to fame and fortune in ministry). It's common for you to welcome stresses as challenges. Unfortunately, you're also open to accepting more stress than you can handle.

Then comes distress in three phases:

1. You realize you can't meet everybody's expectations.

2. You get used to the pressures by working furiously to meet as many expectations as you can with helter-skelter resolve.

3. Finally, you can't take it anymore; you're physically, emotionally or spiritually exhausted. You are busier than ever but never finish projects properly. You forget priority tasks, get fuzzy on what's important and what isn't—you seem to major on the minors. You feel fatigued, drained, disillusioned. You nearly crave seclusion, almost seeking detachment from good friends. You have almost uncontrollable thoughts of "the grass must be greener" and wish that something would just happen to change your ministry, your responsibilities, your abilities, even your spouse. You become one of the thousands of fine youth workers who live in *distress*.

HOW TO BE A HAPPY YOUTH LEADER

Moses was headed for a distressed burnout with all the demands of his murmuring children—all two million of them (see Exodus 18:13-26). Moses' father-in-law urged him to do two things: Get realistic about his responsibilities and limitations. ("This thing is too heavy for you. You are not able to perform it.") Secondly, he urged Moses to adjust the structure of his ministry to accommodate the pressures. ("I will give you counsel.")

Get realistic. Quit pretending that you can meet everybody's demands. Quit trying to be the one who saves the world. Quit posing as "The Answerperson." Quit running as if you have no limitations. Quit thinking you have to do everything yourself.

Some ideas to help you get realistic about yourself and your ministry:

● Recognize God's expectations. Jesus said, "My yoke is easy, and my burden is light" (Matthew 11:30). If your youth ministry yoke is choking you and the burden you haul is dislocating your shoulders, you're carrying a load that belongs to somebody other than Jesus Christ. Can the God who wants you to be "anxious for nothing" (Philippians 4:6) be responsible for running you ragged?

● Evaluate and reaffirm your priorities. Actually write out a list of what and who is important to you. You'll clearly see the need to insist on what's important and to say "No" to what isn't. You'll see that your priorities should be grouped into no more than three major areas (such as ministry, home, schooling). Otherwise, you'll have a hopeless tangle of priorities, expectations and stresses. Learn to manage your time according to these specific priorities.

● Identify your stress triggers. A new job, moving or experiencing changes in your intimate relationships can bring stress. But watch the little items too. Some stressors will be idiosyncratic, nitpicky: When your supervisor asks what you've been up to all day; when your spouse says, "Do we *have* to go?"; when a youth's parent calls to complain, "Chucky hated that last activity"; when attendance lowers; when you're interrupted by the phone; or when the secretary asks for your newsletter column.

● Learn to cope immediately with stress. Practice tension reducers. Repeat exercises such as breathing in slowly, exhaling, holding for six to 10 seconds, then again inhaling slowly. If you can walk, inhale for five or six steps, then exhale for five or six. (A body can't long be tensed if it is mechanically slowed down by a reduction of oxygen.) If you *can't* relax, if you feel chronically overwhelmed by tension, get professional help.

Adjust your ministry. Handling stress has been generally cerebral so far, right? Well, it's time for guts. (Use 'em or lose 'em to peptic ulcers.) It'll take guts to face all those people who have so many excellent expectations of you and for you to tell them that under God you've got to live and minister according to what you believe to be your God-given priorities.

If your family is higher on your priority list than is church or organizational work, start saying, "No, I've got to spend time with my family." Start working with your supervising board or boss to develop a schedule that better accommodates your priorities. Be gracious but creative in pointing out that you will not and cannot meet everybody's expectations. Get gutsy:

- Make it a policy that there will be no youth activity unless a certain number of adults or parents attend.
- Determine that you won't do ministry paperwork at home.
- With your supervisors, divide the day into three sections—morning, afternoon and evening—and only "work" during two sections.
- Weekly take off two or at the least one and a half days besides Sunday, which is probably not your day of rest.
- Recommend that the expenses for your spouse and children be paid for at any youth activity.
- Never pay your own way to anything.
- Accumulate your days off so that after an extended outing you have days to recuperate.
- Delegate everything you possibly can.
- Give your delegates authority as well as responsibility.
- Let volunteers do most of your paperwork.
- Develop friends outside of ministry circles.
- Engage regularly in non-ministry-related hobbies.
- Refuse to have the only available keys to buildings, rooms, vehicles or equipment.
- Get regular physical exercise and eat properly (fats and sugars are stress producing).
- Sleep once in a while.

I know what you're thinking: *If I actually told the board chairperson that rather than attend three committee meetings monthly, I'll send my recommendations in memos and read the minutes, he would smile knowingly and whisper, "Stop dreaming and get back to work, kid."* And he might. But either you're going to live by what you discern to be God's priorities for you or by somebody else's. You'll probably be surprised at how understanding your supervisors and the people you serve can be. But don't expect immediate understanding from them. Sometimes organizations lose sight of the value of your personal wholeness and resort to gauging your effectiveness by your performance.

I once led the youth in a church where I was incredibly frustrated. Frustration always comes when you're responsible for something you can't control. In this case, my ministry schedule was uncontrollable. A better person than I might have been able to handle it all. But it took me years to realize my limits, to start saying "No," to recognize that the structure was actually keeping me from fulfilling God's standards for real ministry. (See 1 Timothy 3:1-7; Titus 1:7-9).

I decided to begin living out my priorities, and either the church structure would flex or it would stride off into the sunset without me. It's still striding well into the sunset without me. And I'm a better man for it. Less distressed. A better minister.

SOCK SOUP

One of my youth's mother hassled him until he was 17 because he wouldn't eat his tomato soup. He said it made him sick. She said it didn't. Even when he threw up at the table, his mother screamed that he was just trying to trick her. Her nagging got to be a serious stress point for him. One evening while the rest of the family enjoyed their after-dinner recreation, the kid sat before a cold bowl of tomato soup. The pressure got to be too much. No, he didn't ax his mother. He didn't break down into a sobbing basket case. He simply again stated, "Mom, I know you expect me to but I can't eat this stuff," and he took off his shoes and socks and crumpled his socks into the tomato soup. The family to this day talks about "sock soup" and "shock soup." The moral? Sometimes you have to do something gutsy or creative to handle stress.

So take on stress. But beat distress by getting realistic about yourself and your ministry and by adjusting the structure of your youth ministry to accommodate your priorities.

ADDITIONAL READING

Stress in the Family: How to Live Through It, Tim Timmons, Harvest House.

Stress Management for Ministers, Charles L. Rassieur, Westminster.

Stress/Unstress, Keith W. Sehnert, Augsburg.

The healthier your
lifestyle—the more energy
you'll have for your multitude of responsibilities in
youth ministry.

CHAPTER
47

Fitness, Diet
And Relaxation
For Youth Workers

BY CINDY S. HANSEN

Dan, a busy youth pastor, works exercise into his daily
schedule by making exercise dates with youth group
members. One-on-one times include tennis, jogging, or biking
rather than fast-food restaurants and pop breaks.

Ken, a health-conscious pastor, has healthful snacks
after each youth group Bible study by encouraging kids to
bring their favorite nutritional goodies. Baked potatoes and
apples, fresh fruits and vegetables have replaced cookies,
potato chips and pretzels.

Another hard working leader, Cathy, makes relaxation
time a priority by reorganizing her job duties to allow for
end-of-the-day free time. Each day now contains time to
read, relax or participate in hobbies.

These three youth workers have found ways to incorporate healthful habits into their lifestyles. The healthier your
lifestyle—the more energy you'll have for your multitude of
job duties. As a worker in youth ministry, you need all the
pep and vitality you can get! How healthy is your lifestyle?

Take a moment to think about how you feel in three areas

of your life: physical fitness, nutritional diet, and relaxation and free time. Rate yourself from 1 to 10 (10 means you feel great about this area of your life, 1 means you feel bad). After each rating, list examples, situations or comments as to why you feel as you do.

Physical Fitness

feel bad   1   2   3   4   5   6   7   8   9   10   feel great

Comments:_____

_____

Nutritional Diet

feel bad   1   2   3   4   5   6   7   8   9   10   feel great

Comments:_____

_____

Relaxation and Free Time

feel bad   1   2   3   4   5   6   7   8   9   10   feel great

Comments:_____

_____

If you rated yourself poorly on the above three scales, take a moment to re-evaluate your schedule and lifestyle. Keep your ratings and reasonings in mind as you read the suggestions in this article. A few basic changes in three areas in your life may help you feel revitalized, refreshed and re-motivated for work in youth ministry.

PHYSICAL FITNESS

One of the more difficult things to do in youth ministry is to find a regular time for daily exercise. Schedules may vary day to day with unexpected counseling sessions, telephone calls and committee meetings—all the more reason to fit exercise in your schedule.

Most youth workers don't have to physically exert themselves much in their daily routines. However, there must be a time to increase your strength, endurance, and flexibility and a means of weight control. The way to do this is by making physical exercise a part of your daily schedule—whether it be jogging, walking, running, biking or swimming.

Some people find the best time for them to exercise is immediately after they wake up; they shower before work so they prefer to exercise first. Others find lunch times work well for exercise periods; they know this is a good way to stimulate blood and keep them alert through the day. Still others find after work is the best time; exercise provides a way to think of the day and unwind. Whichever time fits best in your schedule—make it a part of your daily routine. Exercise should be as natural as brushing your teeth.

● Be conscious of physical fitness during your job. When there is a choice between an active and passive way to accomplish a task—choose the active. Use stairs rather than elevators for errands or hospital visitations, walk briskly rather than leisurely, bike or walk to and from work rather than drive, walk to another worker's office to ask a question rather than buzzing him or her on the intercom, begin meetings with active games or exercises to lively music.

● Bend over, kneel, stretch and reach whenever possible. Stretches at various times during the day help relieve tension and pressure, keep you awake and improve your circulation.

● Combine exercise with visits. One healthy pastor runs three times a week to an area high school, visits with youth group members and friends while he eats lunch, then walks back to the church.

● Combine exercise with youth group activities. Another youth worker has a twice-a-week "Jog and Study." The youth group meets at a high school track. Each person runs at his or her own pace. The exercise time is followed with a Bible study and juice break.

Whichever exercise program you begin, start slowly and work toward a goal. It is best to check with a doctor before beginning any strenuous exercise program. For exercise to be beneficial, you must do the activity at least three times a week for 15 or more minutes. Always stretch to warm up before any exercise—avoid pulled muscles.

Not only does physical exercise help with strength, endurance, flexibility and weight control, it is a great time for personal meditation if you exercise alone. It is also a great way to build community if you exercise with other youth or youth workers. Besides being beneficial, it is also fun!

NUTRITIONAL DIET
A big part of youth ministry is going out for pizza, pot-

lucks and snacks. Most young people's metabolisms are such that they can handle this kind of eating—more so than the adults who work with them. So how do you control what you eat?

● Be aware of what you eat. Create a balanced diet from the basic four food groups: animal and vegetable proteins; milk and milk products; fruits and vegetables; and grains. Although we can get the most nutritious meals with a balanced diet, many of us never have time to make sure our meals are balanced. We grab a hamburger here, skip a meal there. Therefore, it may be helpful to take a vitamin supplement. Ask your doctor or pharmacist for the best supplement for you to take.

● Some overall guidelines are: Eat foods with adequate starch and fiber; avoid salty foods such as potato chips, popcorn and nuts; read food labels and avoid too much sugar, artificial flavors, colors and excessive chemicals; avoid too much fat (trim excess fat off meats, boil, bake or broil—don't fry foods); eat slowly; avoid seconds; avoid late-night meals; and take smaller food portions.

● Keep a supply of fruit juices, fruits and vegetables at your office for snack breaks—avoid candy bars and doughnuts.

● During those committee and council meetings, drink decaffeinated coffee if you have to drink it at all. Better yet—try to get your church to install a juice machine rather than another coffeepot or pop machine.

● If you bring sack lunches to work, keep them nutritious: roasted meats and poultry, no ham or luncheon meats; low sodium cheese, crackers, tuna or peanut butter; fresh fruit or raw vegetables.

● Your church can sponsor "healthy" potlucks. Encourage everyone to cook and bring nutritious dishes. At all potlucks, whether the nutritious theme is stressed or not, take very small portions and try to pick the foods that are best for you. (Choose baked foods instead of fried foods, vegetable and fruit salads instead of desserts rich in sugar and calories.)

● Be a model of dietary consciousness to your kids: Drink milk or juice rather than pop or coffee in front of them. Keep your home refrigerator stocked with juices rather than pop or other sweetened beverages for those times when kids stop by to visit.

● One youth leader encourages nutrition by basing an occasional youth group Bible study on the topic of treating your body as a temple of God (1 Corinthians 6:19-20). She has nutritional snacks afterward: The kids create "healthy bodies" out of pears (for the bodies), celery (for legs and arms), peaches (heads), raisins (eyes and buttons), sprouts (hair). Incorporate nutritious snacks whenever you have a time for refreshments throughout the year.

RELAXATION AND FREE TIME

Rest and relaxation are extremely important. Too little causes stress, tension and eventually—the dreaded burnout. Too much can cause boredom.

● Evaluate the amount of sleep you get by keeping track of the time you go to bed, time you get up and how you feel. Over a period of several weeks, you'll be able to see a pattern develop. As with everything else, balance is the key.

● Balance the time you spend working with the time you spend relaxing. If you find you are working too much and playing too little—try a little creative scheduling. Schedule an hour a day for reading or your favorite relaxing pastime. Some of these ideas may help you if you feel pinched for time.

● Practice saying no. If you feel guilty saying no to requests—be prepared with alternative suggestions, "No, I can't do that, but Sue can." Or, "No, that time won't work, but how about Tuesday at 3 p.m." You be in charge of keeping certain times clear for you.

● Avoid lengthy meetings. Prepare agendas ahead of time and stick to them. Limit the amount of discussion. Table topics that go over the amount of discussion time allotted and bring those items up at the end of the meetings after the other topics are discussed. If you are in charge of meetings and say they'll last one hour—stick to it. Watch the clock. You'll enjoy meetings more, as will parents and committee members.

● Don't think you have to do everything—delegate. Use parents, other volunteers, youth, adults—let others in on the program.

● Plan ahead. Combine errands and tasks. Planning to

visit a person at the high school? hospital? Have to pick up supplies for the retreat? Do the errands in one outing.

Most people think of evenings as relaxation times. However, sometimes evenings are not relaxing because you are thinking of the day's events and tomorrow's things to do.

● Prepare to relax and unwind. Find a person to talk with (wife, husband, friend) and discuss your day. Talk out troubles.

Take a relaxing walk, or a nice hot bath or a shower. Then, read a good book or favorite newspaper. When bedtime rolls around, you'll be ready to sleep.

● Be aware of your biological clock. Some people like to stay up late and get up late, others like to go to bed early and get up early. Whichever you are, realize it and schedule accordingly. If you have to be in bed by 10:30 p.m., plan to begin to relax at least by 9 or 9:30 p.m. Schedule relaxation time.

If you are sponsoring a retreat—get sponsors of varying biological clocks. One early-night youth worker recruits late-night sponsors to stay up with her late-night kids on retreats. (Even for night owls on retreats, it is rarely wise to let them stay up too long—they won't be worth two hoots the next day. Balance is the key!)

● Schedule vacation times—to get a breath of fresh air and find a new perspective. Don't become so busy or so "needed" that an annual vacation can't be worked into your schedule.

● Schedule a daily devotion and prayer time. An important part to mental, emotional and physical relaxation is time alone with God. We tend to get caught up in our days, the people we work with and problems we have. A prayer time is necessary to put all things in perspective, to meditate on God's reassurances. We are told, "Be still and know that I am God" (Psalm 46:10). God cares for us, loves us, wants the best for us, and tells us not to worry. "Therefore, do not be anxious about your life . . ." (Luke 12:22-31). God wants our cares to be lifted and for us to rest in his assurance. "Peace I leave with you; my peace I give to you; not as the world gives, do I give to you. Let not your hearts be troubled, neither let them be afraid" (John 14:27).

Although we know devotion time should be a priority, it is easy to let it slip by. As with exercise, it works best to schedule a specific time to pray and meditate. Whichever time you decide, stick to it so devotions become a natural part of your day.

GOAL-SETTING

Now that you've read the many suggestions for improving your physical fitness, diet or time for relaxation—don't be overwhelmed. You can't try to change your life all at once—that in itself would make you feel run down, tired, fatigued and frazzled! But you *can* work on certain aspects in smaller doses.

● Begin by buying a spiral notebook to use as a goal-setting journal.

● Pick a favorite Bible verse and write it on the first page of the journal. For motivation to accomplish your goals, memorize the verse. Some possible verses are: Romans 12:1; 1 Corinthians 3:16; 6:19-20; Philippians 1:20.

● Look back to your ratings and comments at the first of this article. In your journal, make a list of 12 changes you would like to see—four changes in each of the three areas.

● Prioritize your top three goals—one in each area. Circle or in some way highlight those top goals. These are the goals you will work on first. Word these three goals so that each is measurable and realistic, for example: I will walk to and from work at least three days a week beginning Monday. I will do this for one month and keep track of the days and my feelings in this journal. The next month I will evaluate this exercise and add another day to walk or substitute some other type of exercise should this one not work out.

● Remember to reward yourself when you reach a goal (go to a movie, football game, concert, etc.). Don't be overly hard on yourself when some weeks don't go as well as you'd like. For example, a conference or some other activity may come up and you can only walk one day instead of three. That's okay! Recognize it, record it and try again.

● Keep the list of 12 goals. When you feel you've sufficiently assimilated the first three goals into your lifestyle, add another goal.

Keep track of your progress and feelings in the journal. Listen to your body for the things that need changing in your life and record the good feelings that come with the changes you make. You *can* change from being run down, tired, fatigued and frazzled to being revitalized, refreshed and re-motivated for work in youth ministry.

ADDITIONAL READING

The Caring Question, Donald A. Tubesing and Nancy Loving Tubesing, Augsburg.

Jane Brody's Nutrition Book, Jane Brody, Norton.

My Body, My Life, David R. Ellingson and Darcy D. Jensen, Augsburg.

Whether you are a full-time, salaried youth pastor or an unpaid volunteer, you can deduct many youth ministry expenses.

Lower and Better Manage Your Income Taxes

BY BOBBY O. EDWARDS

I t may seem odd but one of a youth leader's more challenging roles is that of a taxpayer. That obligation affects the amount of time and energy you give to your youth ministry (especially around Easter time if you've put off completing your tax return).

As a citizen you should pay all required taxes. As a good steward you should pay only those taxes required and no more. You have the right to keep your taxes to a minimum. The late U.S. District Court Judge Learned Hand wrote, "There is nothing sinister in so arranging one's affairs as to keep taxes as low as possible." Fortunately, tax laws and regulations provide a number of ways to legally reduce the burden of taxes. Many of these apply to you, whether you're a full-time professional or a part-time volunteer.

If you're an average youth worker, accounting to the government for income and expenses usually falls to the bottom of the priority list. It's easy to avoid advance planning for maximum tax savings. Yet each January 1 begins a new opportunity for planning that can save you a lot of tax dollars.

By not taking some actions early in the year, you assure yourself of paying unnecessary taxes throughout the year. It's also easy to put off preparing last year's tax return. Pressure builds as April 15 nears. It's difficult to celebrate Easter, much less to prepare to lead others in that celebration, when a tax return waits to be completed. Completing your tax return early gives you inner freedom for greater spiritual leadership.

START NOW

What can you do to reduce taxes and make tax return preparation less burdensome? Knowing what to look for and keeping good records reduces your taxes and frustration. I can help you with the knowledge part. The discipline of keeping good records is up to you.

Anything you pay out to perform youth ministry for which you don't get repaid is a tax deductible expense. If you are a volunteer, you should be elected or appointed to the position. The expenses are deductible only as charitable contributions. If you're paid a salary, then the expenses are deductible as professional or employee business expenses.

In either case, the expenses must be considered by the IRS as being ordinary and necessary for the performance of the job. The IRS is usually satisfied if the church has a policy statement in which it states such expenses are ordinary and necessary. Unreimbursed expenses are tax deductible at their actual cost.

It is much simpler to have all job related expenses paid by the church. The second best step is to pay the expenses yourself and have the church reimburse you. (Be sure to give all receipts and vouchers to the church.) The third best method is to have a designated expense allowance.

When the church is accountable for these expenses, no further accountability is required by the IRS. When the expenses aren't reimbursed, claim them as deductions on your tax return. In this case, the burden of proof is on you, so keep all receipts and records. Beginning the 1985 tax year, undocumented deductions will be denied and penalties will be assessed.

AUTO EXPENSES

Whether you are a volunteer or a salaried youth worker,

mileage you put on your auto as you travel for youth ministry functions is deductible. Commuting between home and church is considered personal, not business mileage.

Volunteers—If you choose to use the "standard mileage method" rather than actual cost of gas and oil for your private automobile, you may claim 12 cents a mile. (All facts and figures in this chapter are based on IRS standards at the date of the printing of this book. Always consult a knowledgeable accountant when you have questions about IRS rules.)

Salaried youth leaders—You may claim 20.5 cents a mile for the first 15,000 miles and 11 cents a mile thereafter. If your car is fully depreciated (generally meaning more than three years old or with over 60,000 business miles), then the flat rate is 11 cents a mile. Instead of mileage rates, you may claim actual operating expenses, including depreciation.

OTHER EXPENSES

Your car is usually the major youth ministry expense but there are many others. These include program and training materials such as books, magazine subscriptions, tapes, records and supplies. There are also costs for conferences, outings and training events.

Other expenses which volunteers find difficult to claim but are considered necessary expenses for salaried professionals are entertainment, gifts, dues, continuing education and professional equipment (office equipment, etc.). If you are a volunteer and spend money in those areas, have the church pay for them.

HOUSING EXPENSES

If you qualify, you can deduct the full cost of maintaining your home from your gross income if certain conditions are met:

1. The housing allowance must be officially designated by the church or church agency in its budget, minutes, resolution or employment contract.

2. The church must designate the allowance ahead of the taxing period. The allowance may, however, be amended any time and the new amount applies from that moment on.

3. The amount must be expressed in dollars and cannot

be more than your salary.

Of your total salary, you can't exclude from your gross income more than is actually spent to provide a home. Those costs are limited by the fair rental value plus utilities, furnishings, maintenance, etc. If you live in church-owned housing, you may have a designated housing allowance to cover those costs personally incurred to provide a home. The burden of proof for housing expenses is on you. And you must account for those expenses to the IRS if requested.

Membership to a Christian organization or a church-related organization isn't enough to qualify you to receive the designated housing allowance. To receive the housing allowance exclusion, you must be ordained or licensed and must be performing the functions of ministry in a church or church agency. Church-related or parachurch organizations do not qualify. The one exception is when you are a minister who works for a non-church organization because your church has assigned or appointed you to that position.

OTHER DEDUCTIONS FOR SALARIED YOUTH WORKERS

Many other tax-related aspects of youth ministry can reduce your taxes if you are a salaried youth worker. These include such tax-free fringe benefits as medical and retirement plans, investment credits for equipment purchases, the option to be in or out of Social Security, and the credits and deductions common to all taxpayers.

It is beyond the scope of this chapter to give a complete summary. However, keeping in mind ordinary and necessary youth ministry expenses will help keep your taxes to a minimum.

WHERE TO BEGIN

Plan now—Start now to establish a yearly budget, to get a policy statement listing expenses your church considers to be ordinary and necessary and to get a housing allowance officially designated.

If the budget amounts are not sufficient, if the policy statement hasn't been adopted, if your housing allowance hasn't been designated, or the amount is too low, you need to act quickly.

Get organized—If you haven't started or organized for your next tax return, the sooner the better. Make an appointment with yourself to gather and organize income and expense data. Completing that tax return early will help free your mind and allow your energy to be applied to the more important functions of being a youth worker.

Use this worksheet to help you budget as you set up a record-keeping system.

Ordinary and Necessary Expenses for Youth Ministry

1. Transportation expenses (personal auto and local fares)
   a. Auto miles ____ x reimbursement rate ____ ¢
      OR actual costs (gas, oil, maintenance, repair, etc.) $_____
   b. Parking fees, tolls, taxi, car rental, etc.   _____
2. Travel expenses (out-of-town, 50 miles and overnight)
   a. Transportation fares (other than own auto)   _____
   b. Lodging   _____
   c. Meals   _____
   d. Other (registration fees, materials, tips, cleaning, etc.)   _____
3. Professional expenses
   a. Continuing education (classes, seminars, workshops)   _____
   b. Professional materials (books, magazines, papers, journals, tapes, film, office supplies, etc.)   _____
   c. Professional entertainment and gifts   _____
   d. Telephone, telegram   _____
   e. Professional dues (religious and service organizations)   _____
   f. Clergy clothing (purchase and cleaning of vestments)   _____
   g. Professional equipment (library, office, audio-visual, etc.)   _____
   h. Other: _____   _____
   Total youth ministry expenses $_____

Use this worksheet to help determine your housing allowance and to set up a record-keeping system.

Estimated Housing Expenses
For Ordained/Licensed Ministers

1. Purchase/rent payment or parsonage rental value $ _____
2. Insurance (if not included in payments) _____
3. Real estate/property tax (if not included in payments) _____
4. Home improvement loan payments _____
5. Furniture purchases, repairs, cleaning _____
6. Furnishings (carpet, rugs, drapes, curtains, cookware, dishware, tableware, kitchen appliances, linens, pictures, plants, radio, TV, stereo, household supplies, etc.) _____
7. Utilities (gas, electric, water, trash, non-business portion of telephone monthly service rate) _____
8. Repairs and maintenance _____
9. Cleaning (supplies, rental of appliances, contracted services, etc.) _____
10. Landscaping and lawn care (plants, fertilizers, lawn tools, mowing) _____
11. Legal, bank and title fees (in year of purchase only) _____
*12. Down payment (in year of purchase only unless spread over more than one year) _____
13. Other: _____

Total estimated housing expenses $ _____

*To simplify the church treasurer's bookkeeping, round off the total estimated housing expenses to a figure easily divisible by 12.

Note: While a down payment is includable in the housing allowance exclusion, advance tax planning is highly recommended to maximize tax savings and to reduce IRS audit potential.

Take this opportunity to
wade through those situa-
tions that create the do-I-
stay-or-do-I-quit tension.

CHAPTER 49

Do You Really Want to Quit?

BY JOANI SCHULTZ

How often have you found yourself caught in one of these struggles?

● Things never go the way I think they should. My patience and endurance are fraying fast. I've discovered the aggravating quirk of Murphy's Law: If there is a possibility for something to go wrong, it will go wrong.

● Nothing's fun anymore. The thrill and excitement have vanished with the zing. Situation: boring.

● My noblest efforts have failed to bring expected results. As much as I give my time, energy and commitment—nothing comes back in return. Giving but never receiving creates an empty feeling inside of me.

● I feel as though I don't matter. I sense my presence, or lack of it, isn't noticed anyway. Thinking that I've stopped making a difference, I feel unnecessary and unneeded.

If you've accumulated one or more of these struggles, it's likely that you've also said: "I can't go on! I want to quit!"

These painful words belong to those who wrestle with circumstances and relationships with the desire to "get out."

Being involved in youth ministry—and all of life, for that matter—supplies a variety of experiences accompanied by a number of struggles. Take this opportunity to wade through those situations that have created the do-I-stay-or-do-I-quit tension.

A significant decision is worth important questions. The risky, yet revealing self-examination process provides an excellent opportunity for personal growth. Be courageous. Be honest. Search for your own answers as you untangle uncertainties. Use these questions to begin that discovery.

KEY "QUIT" QUESTIONS

Am I running away from or toward something? This question offers direction. Are you looking for an escape? Are you hoping for a convenient way out of a difficult situation so you don't have to untangle the snags? If you think happiness exists somewhere else, remember—no relationship or situation is trouble-free. Too many people dream of finding contentment by searching for the perfect situation, never realizing that their dissatisfaction is really from within.

It takes work to know yourself well enough to distinguish the thin line between getting out of and getting into a situation. Search yourself. Dig deep inside to unearth the real reason for your desire to quit. Give an adequate amount of energy to confront the issues openly and directly. Nothing is lost by making that extra effort.

If your decision is to continue—you'll feel more settled by aiming your attention to fresh goals in the present situation. If you choose to quit—you'll be at peace knowing you've exerted thorough energy toward your decision.

Let Paul's words in Philippians 3:13b-14 offer a perspective of looking ahead: "The one thing I do, however, is to forget what is behind me and do my best to reach what is ahead. So I run straight toward the goal in order to win the prize, which is God's call through Christ Jesus to the life above."

Am I seeing things clearly? Intense feelings of any kind— anger, hurt, bitterness, love, hate—make relationships and situations cloudy and unclear. Strive to see things from all perspectives. Be brave in analyzing what others are thinking and feeling.

Be just as adventurous in making self-discoveries. Find a

friendly, objective outsider who can help you surface issues you might be overlooking.

In a congregation I once served, a member asked me for a detailed youth ministry report for the annual congregational meeting. Fearful, negative feelings sprung up within me. I thought: "They don't appreciate me or my ministry. Someone is trying to undermine my job." After taking that one comment and ballooning it out of proportion, the picture later became clear: All the person wanted was a better understanding of what I was doing with the young people. Without looking at that comment from a realistic perspective, I had felt the entire congregation was out to get me.

Am I being honest with myself? Wanting to quit lends itself to rationalizations. Check your honesty level to see if it's a me-to-blame or a you-to-blame reason for wanting to quit. Is it always your fault or someone else's when you're unhappy?

Discontented job-hoppers rarely face themselves honestly. Are you afraid to discover the real you? Stop for a minute when you feel no one understands you. Ask: What am I really feeling? Why am I feeling that way? What can I do about it?

Am I willing to live forgiveness? A desire to quit usually involves relationships. Because we're human, we live in a world of brokenness waiting to be patched back together. Our Lord taught us the healing quality and magnificence of forgiveness. When someone wrongs you, can you freely offer that gift? When you've made mistakes, are you able to humbly receive forgiveness from others? Never underestimate the freedom that comes from the gift of forgiveness. It's a healing, relationship-restoring process.

If you find yourself wanting to quit or get out, don't rob yourself or others of the power and privilege of forgiveness. Relationships have the potential of being restored whether or not you quit.

Am I open to finding help? God created us to be in relationships and benefit from them. Matthew 7:7-8 says: "Ask, and you will receive; seek, and you will find; knock, and the door will be opened to you. For everyone who asks will receive, and anyone who seeks will find, and the door will be opened to him who knocks."

That kind of action needs to happen in connection with

God and those he's placed in our lives. If you're struggling, seek support and resources. If you're hurting, knock on a friend's door and share what's going on inside you. If you're wondering, ask for help.

Help takes on all types of creative forms that include: neighbors, church support groups, close friends, paid professionals, prayer and Bible study book resources. You're not alone. After you've asked yourself the preceding key questions, try to keep these kernels of truth in mind:

FOUR POINTS TO REMEMBER

You can only change yourself. You can bring about a difference inside you, but there's no guarantee you can make another person or situation change. Can you live with that?

An inner peace and understanding are born when a person realizes growth and change happen from within. The greatest hope and strength for change come from trusting this secret: "The secret is that Christ is in you, which means that you will share in the glory of God" (Colossians 1:27b).

Be open with your struggle. A sign of strength is knowing your weakness and being open to working on it. There's no need to be afraid of finding help. Trust that a time to grow is at hand. Let these words from 2 Corinthians 12:9-10 encourage you: "But his answer was: 'My grace is all you need, for my power is strongest when you are weak.' I am most happy, then, to be proud of my weaknesses, in order to feel the protection of Christ's power over me. I am content with weaknesses, insults, hardships, persecutions, and difficulties for Christ's sake. For when I am weak, then I am strong."

Admit your struggles and allow God's power to flow through you.

Quitting doesn't mean you're "bad" or a failure. Hopeless as it can seem, wanting to quit isn't the end. Growth comes through pain and struggle. Be positive and hopeful. The gospel offers freedom to start again, to be new. Revelation 21:5 affirms, "Behold, I make all things new!" Celebrate the freedom of newness.

God is at work. God *is* involved no matter what. You, your decisions, your situation, your questions are being used— even the most agonizing choices. God's process of producing growth doesn't stop. Hold on to these words: "God is always at work in you to make you willing and able to obey his own purpose" (Philippians 2:13).

When you find you are struggling and want to quit, hold fast to the certainty that God's love, protection and forgiveness never quit. Trust that promise. Live in faith.

DO I REALLY WANT TO QUIT?

Use this exercise to clarify and understand why you are contemplating quitting. Answer the questions as honestly as you can.

1. How did I arrive at this feeling? (List three to five contributing factors.)

2. What do I think has gone wrong? (Since you wouldn't be in an unhappy situation by choice, what's made it that way?)

3. What would make it better or create an ideal situation?

4. How can I change to get what I want?

5. What are my available resources? (List as many as possible. Include prayer, Bible study, specific people, etc.)

6. Have I been using all my available resources?

7. List a personal goal to contribute to the resolution of the situation.

ADDITIONAL READING

Passages: Predictable Crises of Adult Life, Gail Sheehy, Dutton.

When you say goodbye to
your youth group, your
departure can be difficult.
You can take steps to en-
sure a smooth transition.

CHAPTER
50

What to Do When the Time Comes to Leave

BY DARYL DALE

A youth pastor's average length of ministry within a local church is somewhere between 18 and 22 months. That means youth pastors are one of the most mobile career groups within the United States, ranking just a little behind migrant farm workers. Moving and storage companies appear to be the youth pastor's best friend.

Such mobility is regrettable, because most experienced youth pastors say it takes at least two years to get to know youth and build a trust level. It also takes about two years for a congregation to respect the youth pastor as a professional who deserves its full support.

However, there comes a time when God directs even the best youth pastor to change ministries. What should you do when you prepare to leave a congregation and its youth? Let me help you answer this question by giving you three personal assessment surveys. If you are in the process of resigning, these assessments are extremely important. If you are finding your youth ministry satisfying and encouraging, the surveys can be used for midcourse ministry adjustments that may extend your ministry.

The first personal assessment survey concerns staff relationships.

Staff Relationships

<table>
<tr><td></td><td>Yes</td><td>Often</td><td>No</td></tr>
<tr><td>1. Do you personally respect the senior pastor and the pastor's leadership and decisions?</td><td>☐</td><td>☐</td><td>☐</td></tr>
<tr><td>2. Have you personally met with the pastoral staff each week for two hours or more of sharing plans and goals?</td><td>☐</td><td>☐</td><td>☐</td></tr>
<tr><td>3. Have you built a team of lay people who work directly with the youth?</td><td>☐</td><td>☐</td><td>☐</td></tr>
<tr><td>4. Do parents and the church board know about your youth ministry plans as well as how they can support the ministry?</td><td>☐</td><td>☐</td><td>☐</td></tr>
<tr><td>5. Do you work within your job description, requesting adjustments with proper personnel and at appropriate times in a spirit of servanthood?</td><td>☐</td><td>☐</td><td>☐</td></tr>
</table>

YOU ARE NO. 2

The youth pastor is always in a subordinate position to the senior pastor. Youth pastors who must constantly be patted on the back, receive credit, and be in power positions just don't last. The youth pastor is Christ's servant, the pastor's servant, the parents' servant, and the local church's servant. That may seem distasteful, but it is a fact of youth ministry.

But you, the "servant of all," are in a key position to have direct impact on the church, both now and in the future. You play an active role in shaping today's church through your direct work with the church's young people. To an even greater degree, you are in the process of building and shaping the church of tomorrow. That's an awesome responsibility, far from a second-class status.

YOU ARE A MEMBER OF A TEAM

Youth pastors who try to conduct the youth ministry by themselves create a lay staff problem. They attempt to build an effective ministry upon their personal energies and personalities. But it isn't too long before they start to burn out.

A natural way of dealing with burnout is to leave the situation by finding employment elsewhere.

Successful youth pastors recruit and train approximately one lay person for every six young people in their youth group. This provides each young person with an adult who can personally minister to him or her in-depth. Building a team of youth workers assures the church of a continuing ministry after the youth pastor leaves.

Spiritual

	Yes	No	Not really
1. Are you ending this ministry with the joyful expression, "Thank you, God, for giving me the privilege of serving in this church"?	☐	☐	☐
2. Are you feeling *very* good about the other members of the pastoral staff?	☐	☐	☐
3. You may have been verbally blasted, administratively shunned, and unfairly evaluated, but are you at peace with your thoughts, knowing that "suffering" is a common job hazard?	☐	☐	☐
4. Have you been spending at least 30 minutes in prayer and Bible study each day?	☐	☐	☐
5. Are your words kind and free of criticism as you speak of the people and leadership of the church?	☐	☐	☐
6. Did you attend God's worship services and actually sense God's presence on most Sundays?	☐	☐	☐
7. Did you regularly pray about the young people whom you served?	☐	☐	☐
8. Did you pray about the little things in life, as well as the big events?	☐	☐	☐

Think about question No. 5. When leaving a church, it is important to speak your piece, but do it in the privacy of the pastor's office. Publicly, you should be positive. Never criticize anyone in front of your young people. A few words of criticism can destroy a youth's confidence in the church and permanently scar him or her. If you feel you are not being heard by the pastor, type a written report of your concerns and give it to the secretary of your church board to present to those who need to hear it. If you have been open, honest and faithful to your conscience, let the issues rest.

The last personal assessment survey is a checklist for the departing youth pastor. This is a list of things to be done so that the transition between your ministry and your successor's will be smooth.

Transition Concerns	Yes	No
1. Have you completed an enrollment list which includes the name and address of every young person who has attended at least one youth gathering over the past six months?	☐	☐
2. Have you compiled a list of the activities and programs sponsored over the past two years?	☐	☐
3. Have you made a confidential list of the youth within the youth group who are experiencing special difficulties (to be passed on to the next youth worker by the senior pastor)?	☐	☐
4. Have you listed the traditional youth events that are a part of the church?	☐	☐
5. Have you gathered all the youth resources the church has purchased under your ministry (to be passed on to the next youth pastor)?	☐	☐
6. Have you written a job description recommendation and given it to the pastor as guidance in hiring the next youth pastor?	☐	☐
7. Have you taken the time to personally challenge each young person to take new steps of faith in his or her commitment to Christ?	☐	☐

Personally challenging youth can be a tremendous ministry. As youth pastor, you know the youth well. Sometimes there is difficulty in confronting young people personally to grow in Christ and overcome their weaknesses. A kind word of counsel at the conclusion of your ministry may be easier than at other times and may be the fuel that keeps a youth moving ahead spiritually. Be sensitive to the people in your group who may see your "challenge" as a disguised "dumping" on them as you leave.

If you have a lot of checks in the "No" column, or even just a few in highly significant areas, you may have spotted key issues that have led you into career difficulties. Making appropriate adjustments can serve to lengthen your present ministry or prepare you for a positive ministry experience in your next church. Whether you are leaving or staying in a youth pastorate, the job is challenging. Be faithful to your call, be faithful to your conscience, be faithful to those who have trusted you to minister to their youth.

ADDITIONAL READING

Life Planning, Kirk E. Farnsworth and Wendell H. Lawhead, InterVarsity.

Where Do I Go From Here With My Life?, John C. Crystal and Richard N. Bolles, Ten Speed.